WHAT HAPPENS...

WHEN
GOD
GETS
ANGRY

BUDDY ROGERS

WESTBOW
PRESS®
A DIVISION OF THOMAS NELSON
& ZONDERVAN

WestBow Press books may be ordered through booksellers or by contacting:

WestBow Press
A Division of Thomas Nelson & Zondervan
1663 Liberty Drive
Bloomington, IN 47403
www.westbowpress.com
844-714-3454

Scripture quotations are taken from the Holy Bible, King James Version. (Public Domain)

ISBN: 978-1-6642-9135-5 (sc)
ISBN: 978-1-6642-9136-2 (e)

Library of Congress Control Number: 2023903459

Print information available on the last page.

WestBow Press rev. date: 03/31/2023

CONTENTS

ACKNOWLEDGEMENTS

First, I must thank God the Father, God the Son and God the Holy Spirit for giving me the words, the expressions and the phrases to write this book. I thank Heaven for standing with me and placing words within my thoughts as I wrote.

I would like to express a special thanks to my wonderful wife Margaret Reid, for her patience, understanding, guidance and assistance during the past two years. Thank you for giving me the many hours I needed to accomplish this writing. Many hours that I was not able to spend with you.

As I came close to the end of my writing I was in search of a proofreader. Well, who could be better than a person that contains a great knowledge of the English language. A person that possesses 27 years of experience working in the Space Program at the Kennedy Space Center. A person that helped write many Space and Engineering documents and was considered one of the best English Majors at the Facility. Where could I find such a professional person? Who could that be? Well, I found that person, it is my wife. Lucky me.

Thank you Margaret for the many hours you spent trying to make sense of my writing and correcting my many errors. You are a sweetheart.

Any wording errors or inaccuracies in this book are the fault of the author.

CHAPTER 1

INTRODUCTION TO BOOK AUTHOR

I started writing this book about three years ago. Writing a few pages here and there but not really buckling down and getting the job done. In January of 2021, I decided I would complete the book by the end of the year. By July of 2021, I had completed about 30 percent of the draft. I decided to re-read my writings. What I found was that I did not like the style nor the format nor the way I was interpreting the Bible text, so I started over. Each day I ask God to help me interpret the Bible correctly and give me the words to write. However, any mistakes in this book is the sole responsibility of the human author.

The message in this book will be in the Opinion, Belief and Conviction of the author and his Premillennialism view. The author's view is:

"Christ will come in the clouds to call His people up and remove the church from the earth before the Tribulation Period of seven years. Christ will return to earth after the seven years and reign over the earthly kingdom for 1,000 years of peace."

The printed Bible verses in this book are from the Scofield King James Version. The verse notations are supplied for referencing the actual Bible verses, (example, Genesis 1:1, John 3:16).

I love the King James Version, maybe it is because I grew up reading this version. The Bible is the infallible living word of God, a road map for life and it provides the directions to heaven. It gives joy, hope, peace, love and the breath to live by. The Bible is the Book of life and the guidance to everyday living. When living by the Word, one is living according to

God's will. In the beginning was the Word, and the Word was God, and the Word was with God.

....

Some of the verses in this book will be paraphrased by the author. The author's comments will be identified by being Italicized, as this statement is Italicized, and the comments will be High-Lighted by Dash-Lines ---------- between each comment. The Dash-Line Comments are to emphasize the importance of the Bible verse as the author understands the verse. Each statement stands on its own merit.

....

WHAT THE AUTHOR BELIEVES

....

I believe Christ is without Sin.
I believe God has existed Forever.
I believe Christ is God in the Flesh.
I believe The Bible teaches one true God.
I believe God will bring the World to an End.
I believe The Bible is the inspired Word of God.
I believe Christ was born on earth of the Virgin Mary.
I believe Christ rose from the dead and ascended into Heaven.
I believe In the Death, Burial and Resurrection of Jesus Christ.
I believe Christ will return to Rapture the Church and gather His Saints.
I believe Christ gave His life on the Cross to redeem the sins of the World.
I believe In the Second Coming of Christ and His rule on earth for 1000 Years.
I believe God exists in three persons, God the Father, God the Son, God the Holy Spirit.

....

I believe Man chooses to sin and disobey God.
I believe Heaven is prepared for the Saints of God.
I believe There is a literal Heaven and a literal Hell.
I believe There will be a Seven Year Tribulation Period.
I believe Man was created in the image and likeness of God.
I believe Hell is prepared for those that reject Jesus Christ as Lord.
I believe There is a satan, he is a literal being and he has great Powers.
I believe Man receives salvation by Grace through Faith in Jesus Christ.
I believe Man's salvation was purchased by the Blood of Christ on the Cross.
I believe Salvation cannot be earned, it is a Gift from God to those who will Believe.

....

PROPHECY OF GOD'S BOOK

As the author of this Book, I have taken caution and care to follow the warnings God gives in Revelation 22 about changing the Prophecy of His Book.

Rev. 22:18-19 **For I testify unto every man that heareth the words of the prophecy of this book, If any man shall add unto these things, God shall add unto him the plagues that are written in this book:**

And if any man shall take away from the words of the book of this prophecy, God shall take away his part out of the book of life, and out of the holy city, and from the things which are written in this book.

No one is to add to the Prophecy of the Bible.

No one is to take away from the Prophecy of the Bible.

The warning from God is explicit and direct.

The warning is given specifically to those who tamper with the biblical text.

The Bible can bless one's heart or can curse one's soul if the person is guilty of intentionally altering the Word of God.

The prophecy of the Bible testifies that Jesus Christ is Savior, and this fact is repeated again and again throughout the Bible.

Christ is the Lamb who was slain, and His blood washes away sin, and His blood alone provides entrance into the Holy City of God. And so shall we ever be with the Lord forever and ever.

I have attempted to handle the Word of God with care and reverence.

INTRODUCTION TO THIS BOOK

In this book I will attempt to provide you with a view of the beginning of earthly times and the birth of mankind. I will comment about:
> *The beginning of sin.*
> *God's dislike for sinful acts.*
> *Punishments for sins.*
> *God's saving grace.*
> *What happens when God gets fed up with mankind's sinfulness.*
> *What we can do to save ourselves through Jesus Christ.*
> *What the final destinations for mankind will be.*

You will be able to read about some of the punishments God has delivered to sinful mankind over the centuries. You'll also be able to read what is ahead for the saved and the unsaved people of the world. God has spelled out in great detail what will happen to mankind in the future.

You will be asked to open your Bible and read certain verses prior to my comments. I ask this of you because if I print all the verses that I need then I'd have most of the book of Revelation in this book. Please be patient and we will discover many truths that God would like for us to know. May God bless you as you read His Holy Word and as you read my statements and beliefs about the Bible verses.

The Bible is a book of sophisticated and exact numbers. The number Seven is found many times in the Bible. 'Seven' represents the Sacred Number, the Perfect Number, the Fulfillment and Completeness of Heaven and Earth. It is God's very own number and is associated with Divine Perfection.

Genesis, The first book in the Bible. The word Genesis means "Origin." This is the book of many "FIRSTS."

It tells the story of the world and the history of mankind at the beginning.

The Bible book of Genesis is God's account of the beginning of Heaven and Earth, Mankind's Creation and the Birth of Sin. The Bible book of Revelation is the Judgment of Sin and the End of an Evil Civilization.

....

After Adam and Eve sinned, God's attitude changed toward mankind. Although God hated their sinful actions, He established a plan to save humanity.

....

CHAPTER 2

IN THE BEGINNING, GOD

Gen. 1:1   **In the beginning God created the heaven and the earth.**

Heaven and Earth did not exist before Genesis 1:1.

When God decided to create Heaven and Earth, it does not mean that this was the beginning of God. God has always been. Before the creation of the world of time and space, He just WAS. God IS and has always been.

The Bible begins with, "In the beginning God." There is no question of His eternal existence. Mankind may try to explain away the creation of Heaven and Earth but their explanations cannot override the Word of Almighty God and one day every soul will meet Him.

God lived beyond earth's atmosphere and beyond outer space because these areas did not exist until He created Heaven and Earth.

God did not provide a timeline for the creation of the universe. The creation is a dateless past.

God created Heaven and Earth with all thoughts, ideas and materials for the needs of humanity for thousands of years in the future. Without this care and concern for mankind, scientist today would not have the materials to invent anything or to discover anything.

God created the Solar System with the Planets, the Stars, the Milky Way, the Meteorites, the Asteroids, the Sun, the Moon and the Clouds.

God created the Earth with Oxygen, Gravity, Nitrogen, Minerals, Rain, Wind, Snow, Water, Oceans, Seas and Lakes.

God created landforms of Mountains, Valleys, Glaciers, Hills, Plains, Deserts and Dry Land.

During these creations, God also created Time, Space and Matter.

After the creation of Heaven and Earth, God made everything else by His Spoken Words.
"And God said," nine times in Genesis 1 verses 3, 6, 9, 11, 14, 20, 24, 26, 29. "And the LORD God said" in Genesis 2:18. This is the first time the word "LORD" is used in front of the word "God" but it will be used several more times in the next few chapters of the bible.

God spoke and things came into existence. He is the designer of everything in the universe. He created all things that fills the earth, the skies and the heavens. He created everything that exists including the raw materials we use today.

The book of Genesis establishes God as the creator of all things and the Supreme Being of everything.

Gen. 1:2   **2 And the earth was without form, and void; and darkness was upon the face of the deep. And the Spirit of God moved upon the face of the waters.**

The earth was without shape, without light and it was covered with water. The earth was a mass of complete darkness.

GOD'S SIX DAY CREATION

....

The First Day:

Gen. 1:3   3 <u>And God said</u>, Let there be light: and there was light.

....

God divided the light from the dark and called the light "Day" and the Darkness He called "Night."

....

Each day the light comes toward us at 186,000 miles a second.

....

The Second Day:

Gen. 1:6   6 <u>And God said,</u> Let there be a firmament in the midst of the waters, and let it divide the waters from the waters.

....

God divided the earth from the sky, then He divided the waters in the clouds from the waters on the earth.

....

The Third day:

Gen. 1: 9-11   9 <u>And God said</u>, Let the waters under the heaven be gathered together unto one place, and let the dry land appear: and it was so.

         11 <u>And God said</u>, Let the earth bring forth grass, the herb yielding seed, and the fruit tree yielding fruit after his kind, whose seed is in itself, upon the earth: and it was so.

....

God said, call the dry land "Earth."

....

God had the Earth produce all types of vegetables, trees of fruits and trees of nuts. These are not plants and trees that were already on earth, these are plants and trees that God created from the spoken Word.

....

The Fourth day:

Gen. 1:14   14 <u>And God said</u>, Let there be lights in the firmament of the heaven to divide the day from the night; and let them be for signs, and for seasons, and for days, and years:

....

God presented the sunlight to rule the days and the moonlight and stars to rule the nights. He divided the seasons into spring, summer, fall and winter. He then broke it down to years, days and hours.

The Fifth day:

Gen. 1:20

> **20 <u>And God said</u>, Let the waters bring forth abundantly the moving creature that hath life, and fowl that may fly above the earth in the open firmament of heaven.**

God said, let the waters bring forth its living creatures and let the fowl fly into the heavens.

God created the whales and every living creature in all the waters.

The Sixth day:

Gen. 1:24-31

> **24 <u>And God said</u>, Let the earth bring forth the living creature after his kind, cattle, and creeping thing, and beast of the earth after his kind: and it was so.**
>
> **26 <u>And God said</u>, Let us make man in our image, after our likeness: and let them have dominion over the fish of the sea, and over the fowl of the air, and over the cattle, and over all the earth, and over every creeping thing that creepeth upon the earth.**
>
> **28 And God blessed them, and God said unto them, Be fruitful, and multiply, and replenish the earth, and subdue it: and have dominion over the fish of the sea, and over the fowl of the air, and over every living thing that moveth upon the earth.**
>
> **29 <u>And God said</u>, Behold, I have given you every herb bearing seed, which is upon the face of all the earth, and every tree, in the which is the fruit of a tree yielding seed; to you it shall be for meat.**

30 And to every beast of the earth, and to every fowl of the air, and to every thing that creepeth upon the earth, wherein there is life, have given every green herb for meat: and it was so.

31 And God saw every thing that he had made, and, behold, it was very good. And the evening and the morning were the sixth day.

God said, Let the earth contain its life of land animals and let the animals multiply after his kind. Let the sea creatures and the fowls of the air reproduce and bring forth abundantly after their kind.

God said, "Let US make man in OUR image." OUR meaning there are three persons of the Divine Holiness, God the Father, God the Son and God the Holy Spirit.

God said, We will make man in our image and give him dominion over the sea, over the air, over the land creatures and over every creeping thing on the earth.

God created man. Man was made in the image and likeness of God. But mankind does not resemble God in the sense that God is flesh and blood because God is not flesh and blood, He is Spirit. The likeness part is that man has a Soul and Spirit.

The phrase, made in the image of God, refers to the spiritual part of mankind, not to the physical part. It is our spiritual nature that allows us to communicate with God.

God formed mankind from the dust of the ground and breathed the breath of life into him.

God made the first woman because He knew Adam's need for communion with another human being like himself. Humans desire social interaction with other humans.

Adam and Eve were created with a Soul and Spirit with perfect health, sinless and not subject to death. They were righteous and morally perfect.

The Soul is the part of a human that is not physical. It is different from the body because the body dies. The Soul continues to live after physical death, never dying and living eternally.

The Soul is the center piece of a human being. Every human who ever lived is a Soul and that Soul is existing somewhere today. The Soul is immortal and lives forever beyond the human earthly life span.

With the fall of mankind because of Adam and Eve's sin, the aspect of mankind's likeness to God ended. Sin entered the world and brought along with it, sickness, disease and death.

God create man and woman and blessed them and told them to be fruitful and to multiply and replenish the earth and have dominion over every living thing.

And to man God said, I have given you vegetables, fruits and nuts to eat and this is your meat.

Early mankind and land animals were vegetarians. In the beginning man and beast were not meat eaters. They began eating meat hundreds of years later. God gave Noah and his family of eight permission to eat meat right after the flood ended and they were on dry land.

God created man and all the living creatures of the earth. Man did not evolve from some creature. Man was made in the image and likeness of God. God's creation of man sort of shoots down the idea or theory of evolution.

After six days, God saw everything that He created and was satisfied with the results.

The six days of Creation:
> *Day 1 Created Light.*
> *Day 2 Divided the heaven from the earth.*
> *Day 3 Divided the earth and seas and produced vegetation.*
> *Day 4 Created the sun, moon and stars.*
> *Day 5 Created the water creatures and the sky creatures.*
> *Day 6 Created the animals, land creatures and humans.*

The Seventh Day

Gen. 2:1-4

1 Thus the heavens and the earth were finished, and all the host of them.

2 And on the seventh day God ended his work which he had made; and he rested on the seventh day from all his work which he had made.

3 And God blessed the seventh day, and sanctified it: because that in it he had rested from all his work which God created and made.

4 These are the generations of the heavens and of the earth when they were created, in the day that the LORD God made the earth and the heavens,

....

Heaven and earth were complete and finished. God ended his work and set aside the seventh day as a day of rest. God did not need a day of rest as we think of a rest day because He does not get tired.

....

Those who deny the existence of God on the basis of insufficient evidence should stop and look around. God's fingerprints are everywhere.

....

Gen. 2:7-9

7 And the Lord God formed man of the dust of the ground, and breathed into his nostrils the breath of life; and man became a living soul.

8 And the LORD God planted a garden eastward in Eden; and there he put the man whom he had formed.

9 And out of the ground made the LORD God to grow every tree that is pleasant to the sight, and good for food; the tree of life also in the midst of the Garden , and the tree of knowledge of good and evil.

....

God created a Garden east of Eden and it contained everything that was needed in life. The beauty was breathtaking. It could have been an eternal home but sin came.

....

From the dust of the ground God created man and gave him life. God breathed into man nostrils the breath of life and man became a living soul.

....

The man was given a name of Adam.

....

Adam was a mature young man with great knowledge.

....

God gave Adam a soul, a soul that never dies. The body dies but the soul lives forever.

....

God made the animal world from the dust of the ground and they became living creatures.

....

ADAM IN THE GARDEN OF EDEN

Gen. 2:15-20

15 And the LORD God took the man, and put him into the garden of Eden to dress it and to keep it.

16 And the LORD God commanded the man, saying, Of every tree of the garden thou mayest freely eat:

17 But of the tree of the knowledge of good and evil, thou shalt not eat of it: for in the day that thou eatest thereof thou shalt surely die.

18 And the LORD God said, It is not good that the man should be alone; I will make him an help meet for him.

19 And out of the ground the LORD God formed every beast of the field, and every fowl of the air; and brought them unto Adam to see what he would call them: and whatever Adam called every living creature, that was the name thereof.

20 And Adam gave names to all cattle, and to the fowl of the air, and to every beast of the field; but for Adam there was not found an help meet for him.

God placed Adam in the Garden of Eden and put him in charge of maintaining the garden.

Adam was created in innocence and placed in a perfect environment.

He was told by God of one specific thing he could not do. He could eat from all the trees in the garden except one.

Adam was told by God, "Do Not eat from the tree of Knowledge of Good and Evil. If you eat from this tree, you will die." God was speaking of spiritual death. Adam and Eve took His words as physical death.

Out of the ground God created every beast of the field and every fowl of the air, then asked Adam to name them.

Adam was able to give each animal and each flying thing a name. This alone could make a statement about how intelligent God made Adam. There are thousands and thousands of different animals and fowls. A person that never had a book to read, a picture or drawing to see and never been around these newly created animals until he had to name them, seems God created a pretty smart human.

Gen. 2:21-25

21 And the Lord God caused a deep sleep to fall upon Adam, and he slept: and he took one of his ribs, and closed up the flesh instead thereof;

22 And the rib, which the Lord God had taken from man, made he a woman, and brought her unto the man.

23 And Adam said, This is now bone of my bones, and flesh of my flesh: she shall be called Woman, because she was taken out of Man.

24 Therefore shall a man leave his father and his mother, and shall cleave unto his wife: and they shall be one flesh.

25 And they were both naked, the man and his wife, and were not ashamed.

God took one of Adam's ribs to contribute towards creating woman.

Then God created woman from the dust of the ground using the rib of Adam. Eve was not created above or below man but as an equal to man.

God created Adam and Eve with perfect human bodies then He gave the woman to Adam in marriage. They became as one flesh. This is the first marriage on earth and it set the example for future marriages.

Adam and Eve were living in Glory in the Garden of Eden. They had everything they wanted or needed.

They had daily fellowship with God.

....

They lived in a Wonderland that God Himself made for them.

....

They had a heavenly eternity at their fingertips where they could live forever and ever.

....

Then enters satan, the betrayer of mankind, the evil spirit, the traitor of truth, the enemy of goodness, the prince of darkness, the wicked one that opposes God.

....

Gen. 3:1-7

1 Now the serpent was more subtil than any beast of the field which the Lord God had made. And he said unto the woman, Yea, hath God said, Ye shall not eat of every tree of the garden?

2 And the woman said unto the serpent, We may eat of the fruit of the trees of the garden:

3 But of the fruit of the tree which is in the midst of the garden, God hath said, Ye shall not eat of it, neither shall ye touch it, lest ye die.

4 And the serpent said unto the woman, Ye shall not surely die:

5 For God doth know that in the day ye eat thereof, then your eyes shall be opened, and ye shall be as gods, knowing good and evil.

6 And when the woman saw that the tree was good for food, and that it was pleasant to the eyes, and a tree to be desired to make one wise, she took of the fruit thereof, and did eat, and gave also unto her husband with her; and he did eat.

7 And the eyes of them both were opened, and they knew that they were naked; and they sewed fig leaves together, and made themselves aprons.

Satan speaks to Adam and Eve through the serpent. The serpent was ready to show his power and trickery with his questions and devilish actions. He picked Eve to speak with. Adam was there but never got into the conversation, he just listened.

The serpent befriended Adam and Eve and glossed over what God said they could not do. He presented everything in a beautiful covetous way.

Eve told the serpent that God told them to stay away from this particular tree. They were never to go near the tree in the midst of the garden.

The serpent told Adam and Eve that God wanted them to stay away from the tree because once they took of the fruit of the tree then they would become as gods themselves and know good and evil.

The devilish serpents of today tells us truths and half-truths just like this one did to Adam and Eve.

One of satan's most powerful and effective tools is to get us to question God's Word and Authority.

Satan will twist words, invent thoughts, lie and deceive people into thinking God's Word does not mean what it says. Satan will tell us that there will be no consequences for disobedience to His Word.

God will say, "The wages of sin is death, both physical death and spiritual death."

The serpent told Adam and Eve:
"If you eat this fruit, you shall not surely die. God did not say you'll die immediately. He did not mean right this minute, He was trying to keep you away from the tree because the tree has some good features. Let me tell you what will happen if you eat the fruit. Your eyes shall be opened, you will be as gods and you will know good and evil."

It came down to following the words spoken by God or believing the words of the serpent.

Eve looked at the forbidden tree and saw:
>*A fruit that was desirable.*
>*A fruit that would open their eyes.*

A fruit that was pleasant to look at.
A fruit that would make her and Adam as gods.
A fruit that would give them identity and power.
A fruit that would allow them to know good and evil.
A fruit that would make a person wise, maybe as wise as God.

Adam stood right beside Eve but did not say a word while the serpent was talking Eve into disobeying God.

Eve took the fruit from the tree and did eat and gave to Adam and he did eat. And their eyes were opened. Opened to a sinful world that they had just produced with their sin.

They both fell to the sin of temptation and lust. The lust of want, the lust of the eyes, the lust of the fruit, the lust of being like gods, the lust of the flesh.

Adam and Eve disobeyed God and ate the fruit from the forbidden tree.

God did not enforce the bodily death penalty immediately for disobedience. Many years later their bodies died outside the Garden of Eden.

Adam and Eve just committed sin within the Garden. There is sin within and they see themselves as naked. There was no shame of being naked before sin. Now they try to cover their bodies with leaves.

This event demonstrates the powerfulness of satan for he will perform his trickery of deceptions and misrepresentations until the White Throne Judgment at the end of time.

Adam and Eve betrayed God and brought sin into the world

God hates wickedness. His anger is provoked by sin. He demonstrates His displeasure of the sins of mankind throughout the Bible.

All sin is offensive in the eyes of God. He hates sin yet He has compassion and forgiveness for the sinner while the sinner lives. If the sinner chooses to die in sin, then there is no hope for their eternal soul.

Gen. 3:8-24

8 And they heard the voice of the Lᴏʀᴅ God walking in the garden in the cool of the day: and Adam and his wife hid themselves from the presence of the Lᴏʀᴅ God amongst the trees of the garden.

9 And the Lᴏʀᴅ God called unto Adam, and said unto him, Where art thou?

10 And he said, I heard thy voice in the garden, and I was afraid, because I was naked; and I hid myself.

11 And he said, Who told thee that thou wast naked? Hast thou eaten of the tree, whereof I commanded thee that thou shouldest not eat?

12 And the man said, The woman whom thou gavest to be with me, she gave me of the tree, and I did eat.

13 And the Lᴏʀᴅ God said unto the woman, What is this that thou hast done? And the woman said, The serpent beguiled me, and I did eat.

14 And the Lᴏʀᴅ God said unto the serpent, Because thou hast done this, thou art cursed above all cattle, and above every beast of the field; upon thy belly shalt thou go, and dust shalt thou eat all the days of thy life:

15 And I will put enmity between thee and the woman, and between thy seed and her seed; it shall bruise thy head, and thou shalt bruise his heel.

16 Unto the woman he said, I will greatly multiply thy sorrow and thy conception; in sorrow thou shalt bring forth children; and thy desire shall be to thy husband, and he shall rule over thee.

17 And unto Adam he said, Because thou hast hearkened unto the voice of thy wife, and hast eaten of the tree, of which I commanded thee, saying, Thou shalt not eat of it: cursed is the ground for thy sake; in sorrow shalt thou eat of it all the days of thy life;

18 Thorns also and thistles shall it bring forth to thee; and thou shalt eat the herb of the field;

19 In the sweat of thy face shalt thou eat bread, till thou return unto the ground; for out of it wast thou taken: for dust thou art, and unto dust shalt thou return.

20 And Adam called his wife's name Eve; because she was the mother of all living.

21 Unto Adam also and to his wife did the LORD God make coats of skins, and clothed them.

22 And the LORD God said, Behold, the man is become as one of us, to know good and evil: and now, lest he put forth his hand, and take also of the tree of life, and eat, and live for ever:

23 Therefore the LORD God sent him forth from the garden of Eden, to till the ground from whence he was taken.

24 So he drove out the man; and he placed at the east of the garden of Eden Cherubims, and a flaming sword which turned every way, to keep the way of the tree of life.

....

God only commanded one thing of Adam and Eve, "Do not eat from the tree of Knowledge of Good and Evil."

....

Usually Adam and Eve looked forward to God's visit, but not today. They hid themselves from God.

....

God asked, 'Where art thou?' This is the first question in the Bible. God is still asking that question today. Where art thou? God wants to be our Lord and Savior.

God had told Adam and Eve to stay away from that one tree. Don't look at it, don't come near it and don't touch it. That tree is forbidden.

Adam immediately tried to blame God, then Eve, by saying, "the woman You gave me, she is the one that ate first then she gave the fruit to me."

Eve blamed the serpent and then blamed God. "The serpent told me that it was okay to eat the fruit and since You made the serpent, well."

God placed the serpent upon the ground and told him that he'd be there for eternity.

God said to Eve, "I will greatly multiply your sorrow and your conception. In sorrow you will bring forth children and those children will be born into a world of grief and sadness. Your desire shall be to your husband and he shall rule over you."

God said to Adam, "Because you yielded and surrendered to your wife, cursed is the ground you walk on, in sorrow you shall eat of the crops that you grow. The earth will give you food grudgingly all the days of your life. Food will not grow freely and generously anymore, you will work hard for what you get. By the sweat of your face will you eat. You will do this until you return to the ground. You were taken from the ground and to the ground you will return." God pronounced the physical death sentence for Adam because of his spiritual death.

Adam and Eve lived a life of sweat and hard work until their death. Adam lived to be 930 years old.

God expected obedience, devotion and faithfulness. What He got was disappointments from His created couple.

God created two people that did not obey Him and they sinned. The world has sinned ever since with billions of people falling into the devil's traps.

God drove Adam and Eve out of the Garden of Eden because of their sin. He placed them outside the Garden for eternity. God's original plan was to have Adam and Eve bring sons and daughters into this world in the likeness of God. But now, after sin, children will be born in the likeness of sinful man.

....

Adam and Eve experienced the wrath of their sins, as has the world since that time.

....

They chose their Behavior and they received their Consequences.

....

ADDITIONAL THOUGHTS ABOUT ADAM AND EVE

Adam and Eve were made by God from the dust of the earth. They never went through their baby stage, the diaper stage, the teeth growing stage, the learn-to-walk stage, the terrible twos stage nor the teenage rebellious stage.

No one knows the age of Adam and Eve at creation but my thoughts are that they were made as young adults maybe aged 18 to 22 years old.

When God made Adam, I think He created a mature young adult that was very intelligent and had great knowledge.

I think Adam could carry on a conversation with God. I think he could understand God's requests and could perform the tasks that God assigned him.

It is not known how long Adam and Eve lived in the Garden of Eden before they sinned.

I don't think they lived there very long. For one thing, satan is not going to miss an opportunity to grab one of God's children and have them sin. He is constantly looking and making way toward his next soul.

Another reason I think they were in the Garden a short time is that they never had children while in the Garden. God told them to be fruitful and multiply yet they never had children while there.

When God escorted them out of the Garden of Eden, not only were their souls lost but they were worldly lost because they did not know how to provide for themselves. God had provided for them since their creation.

They left the Garden with only the coats of skins on their backs that God made for them. Even after they sinned and God was disgusted with them, God still cared for them and did not want them to leave the garden naked.

Even if God had sent them on the road naked, there wasn't anyone out there to see them naked. They are the only two people in the world.

No one knows their age when they left the Garden, but I think they were the same age as when they were created. They were going to live forever in the Garden so why age. They started aging outside the Garden.

I think God hated their sin but I think He still loved them. Not enough love to allow them to remain in the Garden because there is a payment for sin. God did not act like the human parents do today when our children leave our protection. We make excuses for them to justify what they have done. Even if we have told them things not to do and they do them anyway. No, God did not do that. Our God today is the same God that was speaking to Adam and Eve and He is sending the same message, "There is a payment due for sin."

It had to be a scary entrance into a world of the unknown. I, as another human being, cannot imagine the pain and fear that Adam and Eve faced. They had no knowledge of a world outside of the Garden. When we don't listen to God, there is coming a day when we must justify our actions.

Adam and Eve had no skills to support themselves. They also had:

No food or water	*No place to stay*	*No house or tent*
No tools of any kind	*No protection from animals, sun or rain*	
No means of making fire	*No knowledge of how to live outside the Garden*	
No cooking utensils	*No cooking knowledge*	
No cooking equipment	*No equipment to till the ground*	
No light after sunset	*No means of killing animals for clothing*	
No friends or neighbors	*No medicine of any kind*	

There were no farmers or people that worked in the fields for food because there were none of those type people in the world. There were only two humans on earth at this time, Adam and Eve.

Are these two people going to be the first cave people? It could be that they were. Very little is known of them after they left the Garden of Eden.

Food would be a concern for them outside the Garden, but let's look at the third day creation. God created the land, the sea, the animals, the day time, the night time, the streams and many types of trees. Some of the trees and bushes produced fruits and nuts and berries. Also there were plants that were edible.

God did not place Adam and Eve out of the Garden to have them starve to death but He did want to show them the results of sin.

Even with no pots, no pans, no fire for cooking or heating, there was fresh food on earth. There was fresh food everywhere because the animals had to be fed and they also ate fruits, vegetables and nuts just like Adam and Eve.

God allowed them to live off what He had created but that would be short term. He had placed them in a position where they had to provide for themselves to stay alive.

No meat eaters at the beginning of creation for man or beast. Meat eating for both humans and animals came after the flood. That was one less worry for Adam and Eve or they may have been dinner for some of the animals.

Adam and Eve:
> *First humans made by God.*
> *First humans to talk to God.*
> *First humans to be loved by God.*
> *First humans to get married.*
> *First humans to have a job.*

> *First humans to be tricked by satan.*
> *First humans to believe satan's lies.*
> *First humans to disobey God.*
> *First humans to disappoint God.*
> *First humans to sin.*

> *First humans to break God's heart.*
> *First humans to be exiled from the Garden.*
> *First humans to feel the pain of loneliness.*
> *First humans to wonder why they disobeyed God.*
> *First humans to have sex.*

First humans to start aging.
First humans to have many sons and daughters.
First humans to not have a mother.
First humans for etc. etc. etc.

Eve was:

First woman to get pregnant.
First woman to give birth to a child.
First woman to feel the pain of child birth.
First woman to be a mother.
First mother to breast feed a baby.
First mother to raise a child without any textiles.

Adam was:

First man to be a provider.
First man to work the land.
First man to learn to grow things.
First man to feed his family through the sweat of his brows.
First man to assume the responsibility of a family.

The first-man-to and the first-woman-to, the lists can go on and on because they were first in every earthly thing.

A little additional info about Adam and Eve, they did not have a Belly Button, (navel). Why? Because they were made by God not birthed by woman, so there was no need to have an umbilical cord.

GOD'S BOUNDARIES AND GUIDELINES FOR MANKIND

God's boundaries and guidelines establishes the rules for mankind to live by. He has specific rules of conduct. These rules are not a condition of salvation because salvation has always been available to mankind by God's grace through faith.

Beginning with the first book in the Bible, God established Boundaries for Mankind's actions and conduct. He set Rules for things that humanity can do and cannot do.

The Word of God is the book of instructions and guidelines for all the living.

These Rules cannot be broken without repercussions. Rules which state: "You choose the Behavior, You choose the Consequences."

THE TEN COMMANDMENTS

....

God further incorporated His Boundaries for Humanity when He gave Moses and the children of Israel the Ten Commandments. These are things that God says do not do. He did not give Moses ten suggestions, He gave him Ten Commandments.

....

Exodus 20: 3-4	**(1) Thou shalt have no other gods before me.**
	(2) Thou shalt not make unto thee any graven image.
Exodus 20: 7-8	**(3) Thou shalt not take the name of the LORD thy God in vain.**
	(4) Remember the sabbath day, to keep it holy.
Exodus 20: 12-17	**(5) Honour thy father and thy mother.**
	(6) Thou shalt not kill.
	(7) Thou shalt not commit adultery.
	(8) Thou shalt not steal.
	(9) Thou shalt not bear false witness.
	(10) Thou shalt not covet.

....

Humanity will choose their Behavior and Receive their Consequences.

....

John 3: 16-18	**For God so loved the world, that he gave his only begotten Son, that whosoever believeth in him should not perish, but have everlasting life.**
	For God sent not his Son into the world to condemn the world; but that the world through him might be saved.
	He that believeth on him is not condemned: but he that believeth not is condemned already, because he hath not believed in the name of the only begotten Son of God.
John 3: 36	**He that believeth on the Son hath everlasting life: and he that believeth not the Son shall not see life; but the wrath of God abideth on him.**

....

The guidelines in this particular scripture states, Believe in the Son of God and have everlasting life, Believe not in the Son and have not life But the Wrath of God.

....

God continues to remind mankind of the Boundaries and Rules He has established.

....

The Bible does not record if Adam or Eve ever repented of their sins and came back to God.

....

These were the first humans and they were created by God's own hands.

....

God created them in His own image and likeness.

....

They walked with God, they talked with God and they enjoyed the Garden of Eden with God. They were not careful enough around the devil and fell into his trap. The devil is after God's people continuously.

....

CHAPTER 3

NOAH, THE ARK AND THE FLOOD

The Bible does not say how many people lived for God from the time of Adam's creation to the time of Noah and the flood. I can only find three men identified in this time frame as righteous and having love for God. Abel, the son of Adam; Enoch, the son of Jared; and Noah, the son of Lamech. They all walked with God and found grace in His sight.

Heb. 11: 4-7

4 By faith Abel offered unto God a more excellent sacrifice than Cain, by which he obtained witness that he was righteous, God testifying of his gifts: and by it he being dead yet speaketh.

5 By faith Enoch was translated that he should not see death; and was not found, because God had translated him: for before his translation he had this testimony, that he pleased God.

6 But without faith, it is impossible to please him: for he that cometh to God must believe that he is, and that he is a rewarder of them that diligently seek him.

7 By faith Noah, being warned of God of things not seen as yet, moved with fear, prepared an ark to the saving of his house; by the which he condemned the world, and because heir of the righteousness which is by faith.

Below are Adam's descendants from the time he and Eve were placed outside the Garden of Eden until the flood came.

Adam's Descendants   Genesis 5:4-32

Person's Name	Years Old When Child was Born	Years Old at Death	Name of Child
Adam	130	930	Seth
Seth	105	912	Enos
Enos	90	905	Cainan
Cainan	75	910	Mahalaleel
Mahalaleel	65	895	Jared
Jared	162	962	Enoch
Enoch	65	God took him to Heaven, Age 365, he never died. Gen. 5:23, Heb. 11:5	Methuselah
Methuselah	187	969 Oldest person to live on earth	Lamech
Lamech	182	777	Noah
Noah	500	950	Japheth

Life is marked by death. These men lived long lives but no matter how long a person lives, there is usually three words that follows their history, 'And he died.'

Noah is the tenth generation descendant of Adam. Methuselah was the oldest person to ever live and he was Noah's grandpa.

Noah had his first child when he was 500 years old and named him Japheth. Later he had Shem then Ham.

When Adam and Eve left the Garden of Eden, God told them to be fruitful, multiply and replenish the earth. And they did, with many children.

Gen. 6: 1-4   **1 And it came to pass, when men began to multiply on the face of the earth, and daughters were born unto them.**

2 That the sons of God saw the daughters of men that they were fair; and they took them wives of all which they chose.

3 And the LORD said, My spirit shall not always strive with man, for that he also is flesh: yet his days shall be an hundred and twenty years.

4 There were giants in the earth in those days; and also after that, when the sons of God came in unto the daughters of men, and they bare children to them, the same became mighty men which were of old, men of renown.

Men's lust and desire saw the beauty of evil and took unto themselves wives and had many children.

As time went by mankind began to multiply and more and more children were born. The population began to double, then triple and then it went wild. People were everywhere and they were all born into evil families. The children followed the ways of their parents and it went this way for generations.

There were no birth control provisions in those days. Children came often and families were very large.

For centuries mankind did as they pleased. They did not worship God or give Him a second thought. Life was to be enjoyed and they did not have to answer to anyone.

Gen. 6: 5-7

5 And God saw that the wickedness of man was great in the earth, and that every imagination of the thoughts of his heart was only evil continually.

6 And it repented the LORD that he had made man on the earth, and it grieved him at his heart.

7 And the LORD said, I will destroy man whom I have created from the face of the earth; both

man, and beast, and the creeping thing, and the fowls of the air; for it repenteth me that I have made them.

The evil people were creating more and more ways of wickedness. Their very thoughts were a continuous action of evil.

God was sorry that He had made man, for man had turned to such sinful ways. Their sins grieved the heart of God.

God said He would destroy mankind, all the beast, all the creeping things and all the flying things for it made Him feel repentant that He had made them. The sins of mankind breaks God's heart.

I'll say this again, God hates wickedness. His anger is provoked by sin. He demonstrates His displeasure of the sins of mankind throughout the Bible.

All sin is offensive in the eyes of God. He hates sin yet He has compassion and forgiveness for the sinner while the sinner lives. If the sinner chooses to die in sin, then there is no hope for their eternal soul.

Gen. 6: 8-14   **8 But Noah found grace in the eyes of the LORD.**

9 These are the generations of Noah: Noah was a just man and perfect in his generation, and Noah walked with God.

10 And Noah begat three sons, Shem, Ham, and Japheth.

11 The earth also was corrupt before God, and the earth was filled with violence.

12 And God looked upon the earth, and, behold, it was corrupt; for all flesh had corrupted his way upon the earth.

13 And God said unto Noah, the end of all flesh is come before me; for the earth is filled

with violence through them; and, behold, I will destroy them with the earth.

14 Make thee an ark of gopher wood; rooms shalt thou make in the ark, and shalt pitch it within and without with pitch.

The story of Noah includes: God, Noah, Noah's Family, the World's Human Population, the Animals of the World, the Building of an Ark, the Flood, the Death of Mankind, the First Rainbow and the Reason for the Rainbow.

In verse 8, this is the first time in the Bible that the word 'Grace' is used. 'Grace' is the goodness of God extended to mankind.

Noah was justified before God by faith and he walked with God. He was a righteous man, blameless among the people of his time.

God chose Noah to build the ark that would house thousands of animals and keep them safe during the flood.

The earth was corrupt and filled with violence. Only Noah and his family of eight loved God and were not like the rest of the world. They were the only righteous people on earth.

The sinful flesh of the earth provoked God to do something. The people had lived this way for hundreds of years and they loved the sinful life style. No one was going to change them, not even God. They ignored God and His warnings.

God said to Noah, The earth is so corrupt and violent, I am going to destroy all of mankind and clean the earth of the violence and wickedness.

God told Noah to build an ark. God gave the length, the breadth, the height and the number of floors He wanted in the ark. He also told Noah that there would be animals in the ark, male and female, along with food for all. There would also be eight members of his family in the ark.

I can hear God telling Noah, "Build the Ark on that dry land over there, away from the water. When it is time to put it in the water and make it float, I'll take care of that."

It has been over 1500 years since Adam and Eve left the Garden of Eden. There are millions and millions of people on earth at this time. People were living five hundred years, six hundred years, seven hundred years, eight hundred years and some even nine hundred years. They were having children for several hundred years of their life.

Adam was able to father children and Eve was able to conceive children for 800 years and there were many sons and daughters born to them.

Gen. 6:17-20

17 And, behold, I, even I, do bring a flood of waters upon the earth, to destroy all flesh, wherein is the breath of life, from under heaven; and everything that is in the earth shall die.

18. But with thee will I establish my covenant; and thou shalt come into the ark, thou, and thy sons, and thy wife, and thy sons' wives with thee.

19 And of every living thing of all flesh, two of every sort shalt thou bring into the ark, to keep them alive with thee; they shall be male and female.

20 Of fowls after their kind, and of cattle after their kind, of every creeping thing of the earth after his kind, two of every sort shall come unto thee, to keep them alive.

God said, Everything on earth will die from the flood waters except the fish and water creatures. Everything that breathes will die except the people and the animals in the ark. God destroyed every living creature that was left on earth.

Noah and his family will be in the ark of safety with God.

Prior to the rain coming, Noah had to get the animals into the ark and he must be sure to have a male and a female of each kind.

God established a covenant with Noah that he and his family will be safe. This is the first time the word 'covenant' is used in the bible.

The Spirit of the Lord caused the animals and the birds to come into the ark two by two.

Noah did all that God told him to do and God was pleased.

Gen. 7:1-3	**1 And the Lord said unto Noah, come thou and all thy house into the ark; for thee have I seen righteous before me in this generation.**

2 Of every clean beast thou shalt take to thee by sevens, the male and his female: and of beasts that are not clean by two, the male and his female.

3 Of fowls also of the air by sevens, the male and the female: to keep seed alive upon the face of all the earth.

God told Noah and his family to come into the ark for their righteousness had saved them. He did not say 'go' into the ark, He said 'come' because that is where God is, in the ark.

God directed the ark to its destination and provided peace and safety to Noah and his family.

Of the millions of people on earth, God could only find eight people that should be saved.

God told Noah to take clean and unclean animals into the ark. Of the clean animal group, take a male and a female of each group and take seven pairs of each. Of the unclean animal group, take a male and a female, but only take two pairs of each.

Leviticus 11 provides an extensive list of the clean beast, unclean beasts, insects, fish and birds.

Gen. 7:4-10	**4 For yet seven days, and I will cause it to rain upon the earth forty days and forty nights; and every living substance that I have made will I destroy from off the face of the earth.**

5 And Noah did according unto all that the LORD commanded him.

6 And Noah was six hundred years old when the flood of waters was upon the earth.

7 And Noah went in, and his sons, and his wife, and his sons' wives with him, into the ark, because of the waters of the flood.

8 Of clean beasts, and of beasts that are not clean, and of fowls, and of every thing that creepeth upon the earth,

9 There went in two and two unto Noah into the ark, the male and the female, as God had commanded Noah,

10 And it came to pass after seven days, that the waters of the flood were upon the earth.

God tells Noah that in seven days He will cause it to rain for forty days and forty nights and He will destroy every breathing creature on the face of the earth. This includes, humans, animals, fowls and everything that creeps upon the land.

This will be rain like the world has never seen. The rain will be violent and will not stop until it covers the highest mountains. The ark will be the only thing above the water.

God was fed up with their sinful lives and He decided to end all life on earth.

Noah tried to tell the people that they needed to change their way of living but they just laughed at him and called him a fool. But he just kept building. Building a boat right out in the desert just as God asked him to do. When Noah was finished with the ark God took over.

God had the animals march right into the ark.

Noah was 600 years old when he and his family entered the ark. The family of eight included Noah, his wife, their three sons and their wives.

Gen. 7:16-24

16 And they that went in, went in male and female of all flesh, as God had commanded him: and the Lord shut him in.

17 And the flood was forty days upon the earth; and the waters increased, and bare up the ark, and it was lifted up above the earth.

18 And the waters prevailed, and were increased greatly upon the earth; and the ark went upon the face of the waters.

19 And the waters prevailed exceedingly upon the earth; and all the high hills, that were under the whole heaven, were covered.

20 Fifteen cubits upward did the waters prevail; and the mountains covered.

21 And all flesh died that moved upon the earth, both of fowl, and of cattle, and of beast, and of every creeping thing that creepeth upon the earth, and every man:

22 All in whose nostrils was the breath of life, of all that was in the dry land, died.

23 And every living substance was destroyed which was upon the face of the ground, both man, and cattle, and the creeping things, and fowl of the heaven; and they were destroyed from the earth: and Noah only remained alive, and they that were with him in the ark.

24 And the waters prevailed upon the earth an hundred and fifty days.

The Lord shut the door to the ark. This means that everything in the ark was secured by God Himself. No man can open the door and no harm can come to those inside. They are secure from all outside forces.

The ark was very large, 450 feet long by 75 feet wide by 45 feet high. With only one person to start the project, it is easy to believe that it took many years to complete. God had to give Noah the brains, the knowledge and the strength to complete a task such as this. It must have taken Noah many years to build the ark.

The ark had three stories and a roof with a small opening around the roof line. It was built to float.

When time was right, God sent the flood waters. Water came down from Heaven as well as coming up from the springs beneath the ground.

The flood waters began about 1650 years after Adam and Eve left the Garden of Eden.

The waters came and the ark began to float. After forty days of rain, there was nothing to see outside the ark but water. They could not see any land, any houses, any hills, any mountains, any trees, any people or any animals. Everything was under water and everything was gone.

The water was about 23 feet above the highest mountain top.

The ark had no steering wheel. Steering the ark was done by God Himself, thus there was no need for a steering wheel. God commanded the wind to blow the ark where He wanted it to go.

No one knows how many animals were placed in the ark but it was as many as God wanted.

Male and female animals and fowls of the air were in the ark. No fish or water animals were in the ark. There was plenty of water for them to live on earth and God was going to give them a lot more.

There were eight people inside the ark besides God. Noah, his wife, their three sons and their wives. God was in the ark to give comfort and to steer the ark to where it was to be parked. Noah did not know where they were going or how to get there. When there is water everywhere, which direction do you go. Noah could only see water.

The ark came to rest on Mount Ararat. The mountain range of Ararat is in the country of Turkey.

Noah and his family walked out of the ark onto dry land a year after the flood started.

They did not see bodies of humans or animals. The bodies had been eaten by fish and sea creatures, decomposed, washed into the oceans or just floated away and rotted.

Every person that came from Adam and Eve are now dead except these eight. They are Noah and his wife, the sons Japheth, Shem, Ham and their wives. The people on earth today are all descendants of these eight.

Lamech was Noah's father and he had other children besides Noah, Genesis 5:30. Noah's own brothers and sisters perished in the flood. They died with the millions.

Nothing outside the ark survived the flood, even the Garden of Eden was destroyed.

God flooded the earth and killed the evil and wicked souls and the world of eight people went on without them.

Gen. 8:16-21   **16 Go forth out of the ark, thou, and thy wife, and thy sons, and thy sons' wives and thee.**

17 Bring forth with thee every living thing that is with thee, of all flesh, both of fowl, and of cattle, and of every creeping thing that creepeth upon the earth; that they may breed abundantly in the earth, and be fruitful, and multiply upon the earth.

18 And Noah went forth, and his sons, and his wife, and his sons' wives with him:

19 Every beast, every creeping thing, and every fowl, and whatsoever creepeth upon the earth, after their kinds, went forth out of the ark.

20 And Noah builded an altar unto the Lord; and took of every clean beast, and every clean fowl, and offered burnt offerings on the altar.

21 And the Lord smelled a sweet savour; and the LORD said in his heart, I will not again curse the ground any more for man's sake; for the imagination of man's heart is evil from his youth; neither will I again smite any more every thing living, as I have done.

....

God told Noah to go forth out of the ark with his family and to bring all of the animals with him. God wanted them to bring forth many humans and animals and to multiply and reproduce often. God said 'go forth out of the ark' He did not say 'come forth out of the ark' so God must have been inside the ark with Noah.

....

Noah emptied the ark of every animal and they marched out two by two with their own kind.

....

Immediately Noah built an altar unto the Lord. He picked the very best clean animals and offered burnt offerings unto the Lord.

....

The Lord made a promise to mankind that He would never destroy the earth again with a flood. He also said within His own heart that He will never do another mass killing of humans and animals as He did at this time with the flood.

....

Gen. 9:1-4

1 And God blessed Noah and his sons, and said unto them, be fruitful and multiply, and replenish the earth.

2 And the fear of you and the dread of you shall be upon every beast of the earth, and upon every fowl of the air, upon all that moveth upon the earth, and upon all fishes of the sea; into your hand are they delivered.

3 Every moving thing that lives shall be meat for you; even as the green herb have I given you all things.

4 But flesh with the life thereof, the blood thereof, shall you not eat.

God was saying unto them, these are the same words I spoke to Adam and Eve, let's see if we can do a better job this time, I'm here to help. Go and repopulate the earth.

Mankind was a vegetarian before the flood. Now God is saying, in the future all animal meat can serve as your food, however, you can also serve as the animals food. You eat them, they can eat you.

Mankind must not eat meat that has its lifeblood still in it. The eating of any blood is prohibited.

Gen. 9:8-9

8 And God spake unto Noah, and to his sons with him, saying,

9 And I, behold, I establish my covenant with you, and with your seed after you;

God showed Noah and his sons a rainbow in the sky and told them that it is a sign and promise to mankind that He will never flood the earth again. This is a promise to every generation in the future,

God set the rainbow in the clouds that all may see and remember the covenant that God made with mankind and every living creature of all flesh.

The covenant God made with mankind still stands today. He will never destroy earth again with water.

Noah lived 350 years after the flood and all the days of Noah was 950 years.

CHAPTER 4

THE STORY OF SODOM AND GOMORRAH

Once again God sees that mankind will not turn from their wickedness and once again He must deal with the situation.

As in Gen.6:5-6   **5 And God saw that the wickedness of man was great in the earth, and that every imagination of the thoughts of his heart was only evil continually.**

6 And it repented the LORD that he had made man on the earth, and it grieved him at his heart.

Mankind continues to commit their sinful ways of life. God dealt with the wickedness in the days of Noah with the great flood that destroyed the earth and all but eight people.Now He will deal with Sodom and Gomorrah and their sister cities.

These are two examples of God's displeasure with the sins and wickedness of mankind.

It grieved God in His heart to take such action again. God's anger is provoked by sin.

God saw a world of sin during the days of Noah and took care of the problem with the flood but sin returned.

He again saw wickedness in the days of Sodom and Gomorrah and took care of that problem with fire and brimstone but sin returned.

One day God will see the world again in its sinfulness and He will destroy sin for eternity and sin will not return.

During the lifetime of mankind, many will trade eternity with God for the pleasures of sin today.

God has given mankind untold opportunities to accept eternal life but many have chosen eternal death.

The city of Gomorrah was so evil and wicked that the Greek name for Gomorrah means "a heap of manure." The people in the outer cities called Gomorrah by its Greek name because of the inhabitants and how they behaved themselves.

The four cities that God destroyed contained thousands of people. No one knows the true number that lived in the cities of Sodom, Gomorrah, Admah and Zeboiim. Historians and archeologists have estimated that there could have been several thousand people. This number is only a guess. However, in the 1960s archeologists discovered a mass grave in the valley of Sodom and Gomorrah that had approximately 500,000 decayed bodies in it. No one knows where the bodies came from.

As God had done in the flood era hundreds of years before, He decided to slay everything in the area. Humans, animals, birds, the ground itself and everything that moved. There was nothing worth saving because of the influence of evil and wickedness in the human race.

This is the story of God's judgment of evil and wickedness. The story of Sodom and Gomorrah and their two sister cities.

God destroyed the four cities by fire and brimstone.

Two examples of God's displeasure with the sins and wickedness of mankind are demonstrated in the Flood of the Earth and in the Destruction of these four cities. The people were sinful, wicked, violent and corrupt.

Zoar was a city within the five cities of the plains but God did not destroy Zoar because of His love for Abraham, the uncle of Lot. Lot went there for safety from the destruction.

....

God hates sin and His anger is provoked by sin. God sees the wickedness of mankind throughout the world but especially in these five cities.

....

THE LORD AND ABRAHAM

Gen. 18:1-8

1 And the Lord appeared unto him in the plains of Mamre: and he sat in the tent door in the heat of the day:

2 And he lift up his eyes and looked, and, lo, three men stood by him: and when he saw them, he ran to meet them from the tent door, and bowed himself toward the ground.

3 And said, My Lord, if now I have favour in thy sight, pass not away, I pray thee, from thy servant:

4 Let a little water, I pray you, be fetched, and wash your feet, and rest yourselves under the tree:

5 And I will fetch a morsel of bread, and comfort ye your hearts; after that ye shall pass on: for therefore are ye come to your servant. And they said, So do, as thou hast said.

6 And Abraham hastened into the tent unto Sarah, and said, Make ready quickly three measures of fine meal, knead it, and make cakes upon the hearth.

7 And Abraham ran unto the herd, and fetcht a calf tender and good, and gave it unto a young man; and he hasted to dress it.

8 And he took butter, and milk, and the calf which he had dressed, and set it before them; and he stood by them under the tree, and they did eat.

The Lord appeared unto Abraham as he sat in his tent. Abraham ran to meet the three men that were walking toward him.

Abraham invited them to stop and have a meal with him before going forward on their journey.

Abraham's wife Sarah prepared a meal for the travelers of bread, meat, milk and butter.

Abraham knew that one of these three was more than an angel, He was the Lord God.

Gen. 18:16-22

16 And the men rose up from thence, and looked toward Sodom: and Abraham went with them to bring them on the way.

17 And the Lord said, Shall I hide from Abraham that thing which I do;

18 Seeing that Abraham shall surely become a great and mighty nation, and all the nations of the earth shall be blessed in him?

19 For I know him, that he will command his children and his household after him, and they shall keep the way of the LORD, to do justice and judgment; that the LORD may bring upon Abraham that which he hath spoken of him.

20 And the LORD said, Because the cry of Sodom and Gomorrah is great, and because their sin is very grievous;

21 I will go down now, and see whether they have done altogether according to the cry of it, which is come unto me; and if not, I will know.

22 And the men turned their faces from thence, and went toward Sodom: but Abraham stood yet before the LORD.

The men ate their meal and decided to go forward to Sodom. Abraham walked with them a short distance to show them the way.

The two men went forth toward Sodom and left the Lord talking to Abraham. The two men going to Sodom were actually angels.

The Lord tells Abraham what was going to happen to Sodom, Gomorrah and the three other cities in the valley. The five cities were known as the "Cities of the Plain" and their destruction is coming soon.

The Lord tells Abraham that He Himself will go into the cities of Sodom and Gomorrah and verify the truth about their sins.

The Lord did not have to go into the cities to verify anything because He already knows everything. He knows all things past, present and future. One of the attributes of deity is being all-knowing.

The Lord is saying to mankind that He knows all that is happening and there will be judgment and punishment of the wicked. The judge of the world is the Lord.

The sins of Sodom and Gomorrah were so great that their sins were threatening the rest of the world.

When a curse is promised for certain action, it will be done according to God's word. God implies that every word of promise that He speaks is true. His attitude toward sin has never changed.

The Lord tells Abraham to prepare himself to lead a great nation and the Messiah will descend from him. The Lord said in Gen. 15:5 that Abraham's seed shall be as the stars of the heavens.

God makes known to man what otherwise man could never know. God is the source of enlightenment.

Gen. 18:23-33	**23 And Abraham drew near, and said, Wilt thou also destroy the righteous with the wicked?**
	24 Peradventure there be fifty righteous within the city: wilt thou also destroy and not spare the place for the fifty righteous that are therein?
	25 That be far from thee to do after this manner, to slay the righteous with the wicked: and that

the righteous should be as the wicked, that be far from thee: Shall not the judge of all the earth do right?

26 And the LORD said, If I find in Sodom fifty righteous within the city, then I will spare all the place for their sake.

27 And Abraham answered and said, Behold now, I have taken upon me to speak unto the LORD, which am but dust and ashes:

28 Peradventure there shall lack five of the fifty righteous: wilt thou destroy all the city for lack of five? And he said, If I find there forty and five, I will not destroy it.

29 And he spake unto him yet again, and said, Peradventure there shall be forty found there. And he said, I will not do it for forty's sake.

30 And he said unto him, Oh let not the Lord be angry, and I will speak: Peradventure there shall thirty be found there. And he said, I will not do it, if I find thirty there,

31 And he said, Behold now, I have taken upon me to speak unto the Lord: Peradventure there shall be twenty found there. And he said, I will not destroy it for twenty's sake.

32 And he said, Oh let not the Lord be angry, And I will speak yet but this once: Peradventure ten shall be found there. And he said, I will not destroy it for ten's sake.

33 And the LORD went his way, as soon as he had left communing with Abraham: and Abraham returned unto his place.

Abraham shows himself as a man that is concerned for others and for his nephew that lives in Sodom. Abraham's nephew is Lot. Lot has a wife and two daughters.

Abraham says to the Lord, Will you destroy the righteous with the wicked? If there are fifty righteous in the city will you destroy the city?

The Lord said, If I find in Sodom fifty righteous within the city, then I will spare all the place for their sake.

Abraham says, I am only dust and ashes Lord but what if I lack 5 of the fifty, will you destroy the city for lack of five?

The Lord said, If I find forty and five, I will not destroy it.

Abraham says, But what if I can only find forty?

The Lord said, I will not do it for forty.

Abraham says, Don't be angry with me Lord, but what if I can only find thirty?

The Lord said, I will not do it, if I find thirty there.

Abraham says, I have taken upon myself to speak to the Lord, but what if I can only find twenty?

The Lord said, I will not destroy it for twenty's sake.

Abraham says, Lord, don't be angry with me but let me speak yet this once, what if I can only find ten?

The Lord said, I will not destroy it for ten's sake.

The Lord allowed Abraham to lower the limit, step by step, until the Lord agreed to spare the cities if ten righteous people were found in the city.

The Lord permitted Abraham to bargain with Him so that mankind will know that the Lord is merciful.

At this point the Lord had finished communing with Abraham and He left.

THE ANGELS ARRIVE IN SODOM

GEN 19:1- 3

1 And there came two angels to Sodom at even; and Lot sat in the gate of Sodom: and Lot seeing them rose up to meet them; and he bowed himself with his face toward the ground;

2 And he said, Behold now, my lords, turn in, I pray you, into your servant's house, and tarry all night, and wash your feet, and ye shall rise up early, and go on your ways. And they said, Nay; but we will abide in the street all night.

3 And he pressed upon them greatly; and they turned in unto him, and entered into his house; and he made them a feast, and did bake unleavened bread, and they did eat.

The two angels that had eaten with Abraham earlier in the day, arrives in Sodom in the evening.

Lot, being the Gatekeeper of the city, rose to meet them. Lot immediately realized that these were not common men but holy men sent from God.

Lot invited the two angels to spent the night with him and he would give them food, safety and a place of rest.

Gen. 19:4-11

4 But before they lay down, the men of the city, even the men of Sodom, compassed the house round, both old and young, all the people from every quarter:

5 And they called unto Lot, and said unto him, Where are the men which came in to thee this night? bring them out unto us, that we may know them.

6 And Lot went out at the door unto them, and shut the door after them,

7 And said, I pray you, brethren, do not so wickedly.

8 Behold now, I have two daughters which have not known man; let me, I pray you, bring them out unto you, and do ye to them as is good in your eyes: only unto these men do nothing; for therefore came they under the shadow of my roof.

9 And they said, Stand back. And they said again, This one fellow came in to sojourn, and he will needs be a judge: now will we deal worse with thee, than with them. And they pressed sore upon the man, even Lot, and came near to break the door.

10 But the men put forth their hand, and pulled Lot into the house to them, and shut to the door.

11 And they smote the men that were at the door of the house with blindness, both small and great: so that they wearied themselves to find the door.

Before Lot's household could retire for the night, the wicked men of Sodom surrounded his home and demanded that Lot give up the men that had just come to their city. This was not a few men calling out to Lot, this was hundreds of men.

The men outside wanted to have a sexual relationship with the two men that had just arrived in town. Little did they know that these were not average men inside Lot's home. These two men were angels and they possessed great power.

The men outside of Lot's home are not ashamed of their sinfulness. They desired men and boys more than women.

They kept banging on the walls of the home and screaming for Lot to bring the men outside. Lot blocks the doorway and begs the men to leave his guests alone.

Lot tells the men to take his two daughters instead of the men that he has inside. He tells them that the daughters have never known man, they are virgins, take them.

The men outside do not want the virgins, they want the men inside. They rush the house to get past Lot but the angels pull Lot inside and close the door.

The perverts outside of Lot's home did not know who they were trying to get their hands on. They did not know that these two men were actually angels. Nor did they know that the two angels had been sent by God to destroy Sodom, Gomorrah and the valley.

Little did the wicked men know that this was going to be their last night on earth.

As the men tried to break into the home, the angels smote them with blindness. Shocked and blind the men stumbles their way back to town.

The women in the four Cities of the Plain were just as evil and as wicked as the men. They were unrighteous, unholy and as sinful.

Gen. 19:12-16   **12 And the men said unto Lot, Hast thou here any besides? son in law, and thy sons, and thy daughters, and whatsoever thou hast in the city, bring them out of this place:**

13 For we will destroy this place, because the cry of them is waxen great before the face of the LORD; and the LORD hath sent us to destroy it.

14 And Lot went out, and spake unto his sons in law, which married his daughters, and said, Up, get you out of this place; for the LORD will destroy this city. But he seemed as one that mocked unto his sons in law.

15 And when the morning arose, then the angels hastened Lot, saying, Arise, take thy wife, and thy two daughters, which are here; lest thou be consumed in iniquity of the city.

16 And while he lingered, the men laid hold upon his hand, and upon the hand of his wife, and upon the hand of his two daughters; the LORD being merciful unto him: and they brought him forth, and set him without the city.

THE ANGELS TOLD 'LOT' TO LEAVE SODOM

The two angels told Lot to gather up his wife, daughters and his future sons-in-law and leave Sodom as fast as he could, Lot's daughters were not married.

The Lord sent the two angels to Sodom to destroy the city as well as the other wicked cities in the valley.

Lot asked the two future sons-in-laws to come with him and his family. They refused to go because they loved the Sodom life style more than their future marriage to Lot's daughters. They remained in Sodom and they both died when the city was destroyed.

The next day the angels were rushing the Lot family out of Sodom. Lot was dragging around at his own pace when the angels put their hands on the family and placed them outside the city.

Gen, 19:17-23

17 And it came to pass, when they had brought them forth abroad, that he said, Escape for thy life; look not behind thee, neither stay thou in all the plain; escape to the mountain, lest thou be consumed.

18 And Lot said unto them, Oh, not so, my Lord:

19 Behold now, thy servant hath found grace in thy sight, and thou hast magnified thy mercy, which thou hast shewed unto me in saving my life; and I cannot escape to the mountain, lest some evil take me, and I die:

20 Behold now, this city is near to flee unto, and it is a little one: Oh, let me escape thither, (is it not a little one?) and my soul shall live.

21 And he said unto him, See, I have accepted thee concerning this thing also, that I will not overthrow this city, for the which thou hast spoken.

22 Haste thee, escape thither; for I cannot do anything till thou be come thither. Therefore the name of the city was called Zoar.

23 The sun was risen upon the earth when Lot entered into Zoar.

One of the angels told Lot, escape with your life, do not look behind you, do not stay in the valley, run to the mountains or you may be consumed with the cities.

The Lot family members were told to not look back at Sodom no matter what they heard or what they felt was going on, just keep going and looking forward.

The Lord was holding the destruction of the valley until Lot's family was safely away from Sodom and up in the mountains.

After all that the angels had done for Lot, Lot had changed his mind and did not want to go to the mountains because there may be evil there and evil may overtake him and kill him.

Lot wanted to go to the little city in the valley named Zoar which is several miles from Sodom.

The angels agree to let him go there with his family. The Lord will not destroy Zoar because of His promise to Abraham that Lot would be spared.

Lot had to hurry and get away from Sodom because he is holding up the destruction of the four Cities of the Plain.

It was early morning when Lot and his family entered the town limits of Zoar.

Gen. 19:24-28

24 Then the LORD rained upon Sodom and upon Gomorrah brimstone and fire from the LORD out of heaven;

25 And he overthrew those cities, and all the plain, and all the inhabitants of the cities, and that which grew upon the ground.

26 But his wife looked back from behind him, and she became a pillar of salt.

27 And Abraham gat up early in the morning to the place where he stood before the LORD:

28 And he looked toward Sodom and Gomorrah, and toward all the land of the plain, and beheld, and, lo, the smoke of the country went up as the smoke of a furnace.

At the moment Lot was safe, God rained down fire and Brimstone from heaven upon the cities of Sodom, Gomorrah, Admah and Zeboiim.

The word Brimstone, means "the stone that burns." The stone is yellow in color. When the stone is exposed to the environment, it is harmless. If you put a flame to the stone, it burns more powerful than gasoline. The fumes from burning brimstone are toxic and harmful to all breathing humans and animals.

Today we call the stone material Sulfur or Sulphur and we use it safely in many products. Brimstone is converted into sulfuric acid and is used in auto batteries and tires, fertilizer, detergent, paint, rayon and so forth.

Breathing Sulfur can cause suffocation. Suffocation was probably realized during the destruction of the cities.

During the destruction of Sodom, Lot's wife wanted to see what was happening to her city and she turned to look back and God turned her into a pillar of salt. She had been warned not to look back but she did anyway. Lot and his two daughters continued into the city of Zoar.

Sodom and Gomorrah were legendary cities in those days. Even today their names are referenced as a symbol of sin and wickedness.

The Bible is clear that sexual sin behavior was the outward sin for which the four cities were destroyed. God considers all sexual sin offensive and disgusting.

This judgment parallels the Great Flood when God destroyed the entire world because of sin. He saved eight people to start a new generation, now He sees how their generation turned out, sin, sin, sin. God now destroys a specific area because of their wickedness.

The area that God destroyed in the valley was 193 square miles. He destroyed every building, every man, every woman, every child, every animal, every crop, every tree, and every living and non-living thing in that area.

The valley was so destroyed that it has been rendered useless for hundreds of years.

When Abraham looked toward Sodom and the Cities of the Plain, he saw nothing that looked like a city. The cities were as smoke of a furnace. The heat was so intense that everything had melted.

Was it meteor showers or flaming asteroid? It does not matter what it's called, it was sent from Heaven to wipe out a civilization that continued to flaunt their wickedness in the face of God.

Some scientist and archaeologist that have reviewed the remains of Sodom, have concluded that the heat that God sent to the valley may have been as hot as the surface of the sun. They believe it would have to be that hot to burn the earth to the degree that it was left after the fires.

No one knows how many people lived and died in the four city area. The fire that God sent burned everything to an ash. A rock burns to an ash at 2400 degree Fahrenheit. Flesh and bone burns to an ash at 1800 to 2100 degree Fahrenheit, as cremation is performed. The surface of the sun is 10,000 degree Fahrenheit.

All of this destruction could have been prevented if just ten righteous people lived in Sodom.

....

There may have been other incidents like the Flood and the destruction of the Cities of the Plain that God did not allow to be recorded. However, these two incidents should get the attention of mankind. God will only allow so much sin on His earth before He does something about it.

....

These biblical warnings were placed in the Bible that we may learn from them and not allow ourselves to be placed in a position where God has to perform divine punishment upon us.

....

As far as Lot is concerned, he left Zoar and went into the mountains with his two daughters. After Genesis Chapter 19, the Bible does not record any future actions or recognition of Lot. He is not written about or heard from again.

....

CHAPTER 5

INTRODUCTION TO THE BOOK OF REVELATION

John, the writer of Revelation, is exiled on the Isle of Patmos because of his faith in Jesus Christ. He is inspired by the Holy Spirit to write what he sees and hears. Christ will use John as His Instrument to write about the Past, the Present and the Future.

The main purpose of the Book of Revelation is to provide the setting for the Revelation of Jesus Christ.

The book is filled with mysteries about the great events that are to come. God gives His final warning that the world will end and judgments will be given to mankind. Revelation gives us a brief glimpse of heaven and its glories. It takes us from the rapture of the church through the final eternal judgments.

Revelation also gives us a glimpse of heaven and all of the glories that awaits the children of God. It gives the Christians an inspirational look at the New Heaven and the New Earth and what will take place on earth prior to that time. The book highlights God's promises to the saints, they will live with Jesus Christ in the Promise Land forever and ever.

This book provides a look into the future of the Non-Christians. The future they will face after the Rapture of the Church. Revelation outlines the seven year tribulation period with all its struggles, sufferings and sorrows right down to the final judgment of mankind.

The book describes the fall of satan and the finality he, his angels and unbelievers will face for eternity. It foretells the judgments that are coming.

The Bible is the only book in the world that gives a preview of the future. God the Father, God the Son and God the Holy Spirit all had a part in recording the facts in the book of Revelation.

Throughout the Bible God has given us references of end times and the future of mankind. I commend the Christians who think about Heaven in all of its glories and look forward to the coming of the Lord. My heart cries for the person who never thinks about Heaven or about hell or about the hereafter. Revelation is God's last warning that the world will surely end and judgment will be certain and final.

God has been longsuffering with the evils of mankind. One day He will reach His limit and unleash His anger on the world.

Mankind will see the wrath of God that is unbelievable.

God's forth coming wrath is not something that can be laughed off, dismissed, ignored, denied, denounced, rejected or disregarded. This is serious and destruction is on its way.

God did not create us to have a lifetime of sin. We are here to prepare for eternity. At sometime in the future the body will die but the soul will live forever.

We are made by God for God. Life will never have significance until we realize this fact.

The closer we come to God, the smaller everything else becomes. The closer we get to Him, the closer He gets to us.

There's more to life than just here and now. The way we see our life shapes our life.

Days on earth are as an ocean wave, here one moment then gone forever.

It is impossible for the human mind to comprehend or visualize the judgments and devastations that will be poured out upon the earth and its people during the seven year tribulation period.

In the book of Revelation, Christ is presented as:
> *The Judge.*
> *The Bridegroom.*
> *The King of kings.*
> *The Lord of lords.*
> *The Faithful and True.*
> *The Alpha and Omega.*
> *The First and the Last.*
> *The Prince of the kings.*
> *The Lamb that was slain.*

Christ is seen in relationship to time as, He who was, He who is, and He who is to come again.

Proverbs 1:7   **The fear of the LORD is the beginning of knowledge: but fools despise wisdom and instruction.**

Mankind do not fear Him because most do not know Him or believe Him.

I pray that the messages in this book will be delivered to receiving Eyes, Ears, Minds, Hearts and Souls.

To better Understand, Comprehend and Interpret the Book of Revelation, one needs to appreciate and be sensitive to the facts of what happens to the Soul of man when death comes.

If a person is Saved,
the Soul goes directly to Heaven when he or she dies, the body goes to the grave. This person is redeemed and reclaimed by the blood of Jesus Christ.

The word 'Saved' meaning that a person accepts Jesus Christ as his or her Lord and Savior.

If a person is Not Saved,
the Soul goes directly to hell when he or she dies, the body goes to the grave. This person is unredeemed and unclaimed by the blood of Jesus Christ.

The word 'Not Saved' meaning that a person rejects Jesus Christ as his or her Lord and Savior.

Rom 10:9-11   **That if thou shalt confess with thy mouth the Lord Jesus, and shalt believe in thine heart that God hath raised him from the dead, thou shalt be saved.**

For with the heart man believeth unto righteousness; and with the mouth confession is made unto salvation.

For the scripture saith, Whosoever believeth on him shall not be ashamed.

Only the Word of God will stand at the Judgment and the only way to God is through Jesus Christ.

THE BOOK OF REVELATION

Author: Apostle John, One of the Disciples of Jesus.
John is called 'The Disciple whom Jesus loved.'
John wrote 5 of the 27 books in the New Testament.

John Wrote: *The Gospel of John.*
The First Epistle of John.
The Second Epistle of John.
The Third Epistle of John.
Revelation.

In these five Bible books, John wrote about:
The Divinity of Christ.
The Holiness of Christ.
The Godhead of Christ.
The Authority of Christ.
The Equality of Christ.
The Sinless Nature of Christ.

The Security of Christ.
The Reliability of Christ.
The Love of Christ.

The Life of Christ.
The Promises of Christ.
The Assurances of Christ.

The Guarantees of Christ.
The Crucifixion of Christ.
The Death of Christ.
The Resurrection of Christ.
The Revelation of Christ.
The Return of Christ.
The Judgments of Christ.

THE THREE DIVISIONS OF REVELATION

....

The Past .... things that have been seen.
The Present ... things that are being seen currently.
The Future .... things that are approaching and will be forthcoming.

....

Chapters 1-3	*Conditions of the Church Age and the messages to the Churches of today and forward.*

....

Chapters 4-18	*Rapture of the Church*
	Seven Year Tribulation Period
	Opening of the Seven-Sealed Scroll
	The first Six Seals opened
	Jews and Gentiles saved during the Tribulation
	Seven Trumpet Judgment
	Ministry of the Two Witnesses
	The Seventh Trumpet
	Seven Bowl (Vial) Judgments

....

Chapters 19-22	*Second Coming of Christ*
	Battle of Armageddon
	Millennium, One Thousand Years of Peace
	Satan bound in the Bottomless Pit for 1000 years
	White Throne Judgment, Final Judgment of Unsaved
	Holy City, New Jerusalem

....

Revelation is filled with:
> *The Promises of the Bible.*
> *The Puzzles of the Future.*
> *The Secrets of the Heavens.*
> *The Wonders of the Journey.*
> *The Mysteries of the Afterlife.*
> *The Assuredness of the Judgments.*
> *The Authority of the Holy Scripture.*
> *The Realization of the Heavenly Father.*
> *The Termination of the Sinful Civilization.*

> *The Splendors of Paradise.*
> *The Finalization of Eternity.*
> *The Security of Jesus Christ.*
> *The Conclusion of Wickedness.*

The Assurance of Sinless Lives.
The Foretelling of Sin and Hellfire.
The Endlessness of Forever and Ever.
The Accumulation of End Time Truths.
The Wrathfulness and Condemnation of God.

A normal interpretation of the Revelation Scriptures mean:
It makes sense to you.
You understand it in its normal sense.
You take the Word as it is written as the truth.
You believe that Jesus told John what to write.

The Key to understanding Revelation is to interpret it as literally as possible. It Says what it Means and Means what it Says. We are not to look for other meanings of a sentence if the natural meaning makes sense.

Some of the recorded events in the book of Revelation happened in the past, others will happen in the future. These are things that will happen at the end of time, but not necessarily in the order that God allowed John to see, to hear and to write down.

The first 3 chapters of Revelation is dedicated to the Church Ages of the Past, Present and Future.

Read Rev. 1:4

Seven churches portraying the entire church age.

Portraying grace and peace and the seven Spirits of God.

Isaiah 11:2 **And the spirit of the LORD shall rest upon him, the spirit of wisdom and understanding, the spirit of counsel and might, the spirit of knowledge and of the fear of the LORD;**

Old Testament Isaiah relates the seven Spirits of God.
The Spirit of the Lord.
The Spirit of Wisdom.
The Spirit of Understanding.

The Spirit of Counsel.
The Spirit of Might (Power).
The Spirit of Knowledge.
The Spirit of the Fear of the Lord.

CHAPTER 6

DESCRIPTION OF JESUS CHRIST IN HEAVEN

Rev. 1:13-20

And in the midst of the seven candlesticks one like unto the Son of man, clothed with a garment down to the foot, and girt about the paps with a golden girdle.

His head and his hairs were white like wool, as white as snow; and his eyes were as a flame of fire;

And his feet like unto fine brass, as if they burned in a furnace; and his voice as the sound of many waters.

And he had in his right hand seven stars: and out of his mouth went a sharp twoedged sword: and his countenance was as the sun shineth in his strength.

And when I saw him, I fell at his feet as dead. And he laid his right hand upon me, saying unto me, Fear not; I am the first and the last:

I am he that liveth, and was dead; and, behold, I am alive for evermore, Amen; and have the keys of hell and of death.

Write the things which thou hast seen, and the things which are, and the things which shall be hereafter;

The mystery of the seven stars which thou sawest in my right hand, and the seven golden candlesticks. The seven stars are the angels of the seven churches: and the seven candlesticks which thou sawest are the seven churches.

Rev. 1:11, 19	*Christ commands John to write in a book, what he sees and hears.*
Rev. 2 - Rev 3	*John writes letters to the Seven Churches*
Rev. 2:1-7	*John writes to church 1, Ephesus* *Church at the end of the Apostolic* *The Loveless Church*
Rev. 2:8-11	*John writes to church 2, Smyrna* *Church under oppression and persecution* *The Persecuted Church*
Rev. 2:12-17	*John writes to church 3, Pergamos* *Church settled in society and the worldly activities* *The Compromising Church*
Rev. 2:18-29	*John writes to church 4, Thyatira* *Church devoted to the worship of idols* *The Corrupt Church*
Rev. 3:1-6	*John writes to church 5, Sardis* *Church without life, but having a few believers* *The Dead Church*
Rev. 3:7-13	*John writes to church 6, Philadelphia* *Church of renewal and revival* *The Faithful Church*

Rev. 3:14-22   *John writes to church 7, Laodicea*
                        Church in its final state of disloyalty and defection
                        The Lukewarm Church

The Lord loves His church and expects His church to preach salvation throughout the world and make Jesus Christ known to all.

The Churches will not be able to escape the responsibilities that were assigned to them.

God will hold His churches accountable.

Rev. 3:20   *Jesus says, "Behold, I stand at the door and knock."*

Rev. 3:22   *Holy Spirit says, "He who has an ear, let him hear."*

God is saying to mankind, I have known you from the beginning of time:
    Before you were even Conceived.
    Before you had your first Heart Beat.
    Before you took your First Breath.
    Before you were able to See.
    Before you were able to Crawl.
    Before you took your First Step.

I have seen:
    All your Sins.
    All your Fears.
    All your Pains.
    All your Hope.
    All your Tears.

I have seen:
    All your Doubts.
    All your Failures.
    All your Wounds.
    All your Dreams.
    All your Sorrows.

I have seen:
>   *All your Burdens.*
>   *All your Mourning.*
>   *All your Emotions.*
>   *All your Emptiness.*
>   *All your Discretions.*

I have seen:
>   *All your Weaknesses.*
>   *All your Disappoints.*
>   *All your Heartbreaks.*
>   *Yet I still have an everlasting love for you.*

God says, "Come unto me and I will not turn you away."

"Come out of your darkness and I will forgive you and take you with me to the Promise Land."

"For in that day, you will be mine and I will be yours forever."

God's Word is Powerful, Clear, Distinct, Compelling and Authoritative.

This is the perfect and final plan of God for humanity.

A redeemed soul has nothing to fear from God's judgments of the world.

After Revelation 3:22, the Church no longer appears on earth.

THINGS PRESENT TODAY

There are wars and rumors of wars.

Nations are rising against nations and kingdoms against kingdoms.

Many new diseases are appearing on earth.

Evil is increasing in the world.

Man is against man in the name of religion.

Mankind has developed alternate lifestyles and the styles are accepted as normal.

The world is possessed with self-pleasure and self-indulgence.

Morals and spiritual foundations are disappearing.

The world is producing a generation of people that look to the government for the answers to their problems. These people have an 'entitlement' state of mind.

The followers of Jesus Christ are seeing their Christian freedoms disappearing.

Great military powers are within nations today and these nations have weapons that can destroy all life on earth.

A great percentage of mankind Does Not believe that:
> *The Rapture is coming.*
> *The Seven Year Tribulation is coming.*
> *The Judgments of God are coming.*
> *The Day of Final Judgment is coming.*

THINGS FUTURE

....

This part of the Book will mostly address the Time Span from:
  The Rapture of the Church,
  Through the Seven Year Tribulation and
  Forward.

....

Matt. 24:36-42 **But of that day and hour knoweth no man, no, not the angels of heaven, but my Father only.**

       But as the days of Noah were, so shall also the coming of the Son of man be.

       For as in the days that were before the flood they were eating and drinking, marrying and giving in marriage, until the day that Noah entered into the ark,

       And knew not until the flood came, and took them all away; so shall also the coming of the Son of man be.

       Then shall two be in the field; the one shall be taken, and the other left.

       Two women shall be grinding at the mill; the one shall be taken, and the other left.

       Watch therefore: for ye know not what hour your Lord doth come.

....

As in the day of Noah, God will only let mankind go so far before He says again, "Mankind you have gone too far."

....

The Rapture of the Church will occur when God says it will.

....

Jesus will descend from Heaven and collect His Church of born again Christians.

....

The earth will be left without the Church and without the Holy Spirit.

....

The gap of time between the Crucifixion of Jesus Christ and when Christ will come to Rapture the Church of believers, is only known by God Himself.

Not even the Angels in Heaven nor the Son of God knows when that will be. Only God will make that decision.

The next Great event in Christianity is the RAPTURE of the Church.

The Rapture event occurs following the messages to the Churches in Revelation 3.

The Rapture means that the Church is taken out of earth to forever be with the Lord.

Heb. 9:27   **And it is appointed unto men once to die, but after this the judgment.**

Due to the fall of mankind, everyone is under the sentence of death.

All are dead spiritually and are separated from God.

Accept Christ as Savior or Reject Christ as Savior, all will face Him as Judge. All will give account of themselves.

Christ is the Savior but He is also the Judge. All the saved and the unsaved will be judged by Christ.

Reject Christ as Savior and the judgment will be Hell.

Accept Christ as Savior and the judgment will be Heaven.

Christ on the Cross is the only answer for sin.

Starting with the Rapture of the Church through the end of the Bible, these are NOT things that MAY happen, these are things that WILL happen, just as sure as You Breathe to Stay Alive.

CHAPTER 7

THE RAPTURE OF THE CHURCH

I Cor. 15:51-52   **Behold, I shew you a mystery; We shall not all sleep, but we shall all be changed.**

                       In a moment, in the twinkling of an eye, at the last trump: for the trumpet shall sound, and the dead shall be raised incorruptible, and we shall be changed.

At earthly death, the soul of a Christian instantly goes to Heaven to be with the Lord.

The body goes to the grave.

At the time of the Rapture, many Christians will be alive.

Both the dead Christians and the live Christians will have their bodies changed.

How long will it take to be changed? In a moment, in the twinkling of an eye.

The dead will rise with no sin nature and all will be given Glorified Bodies.

This is the end of the Church age on earth.

I Thes. 4:14-17   **For if we believe that Jesus died and rose again, even so them also which sleep in Jesus will God bring with him.**

For this we say unto you by the word of the Lord, that we which are alive and remain unto the coming of the Lord shall not prevent them which are asleep.

For the Lord himself shall descend from Heaven with a shout, with the voice of the archangel, and with the trump of God: and the dead in Christ shall rise first:

Then we which are alive and remain shall be caught up together with them in the clouds, to meet the Lord in the air: and so shall we ever be with the Lord.

The Foundation of Christianity is the Death and Resurrection of Christ.

The Resurrection of Christ guarantees the Resurrection of all Saints.

The Resurrection process is in the hands of God.

At the Rapture, Christ will replace the physical body with a Glorified Body.

Christ will bring each soul and spirit of those in Heaven with Him as He unites the soul and spirit with a Glorified Body.

With the Glorified Body, it will be impossible to sin.

The dead in Christ, born again Christians, shall rise first.

The living saints will not precede or go before the dead saints.

Those which are alive will be caught up together with the resurrected dead in the clouds and meet the Lord in the air.

Christ will not come all the way to earth.

Only the saints will be able to see Christ.

Christians that are alive and on earth at this time will escape the Seven Year Tribulation.

This is the Rapture of the Church, not the Second Coming of Christ.

THE SAINTS STAND BEFORE THE JUDGMENT SEAT OF CHRIST

II Cor. 5:10	For we must all appear before the Judgment Seat of Christ, that every one may receive the things done in his body according to that he hath done, whether it is good or bad.

Only church-age saints will appear at this judgment.

The saints will stand before the Judgment Seat of Christ and be judged.

The judgment will take place in Heaven right after the Rapture.

The purpose of this judgment is to examine a Christian's total life. A review of each life for the Lord will take place. It's a time of reward, not punishment.

Roman 14:10-12	But why dost thou judge thy brother? or why dost thou set at nought thy brother? for we shall all stand before the judgment seat of Christ.
	For it is written, As I live, saith the Lord, every knee shall bow to me, and every tongue shall confess to God.
	So then every one of us shall give account of himself to God.

All saints will be judged at this time, not for their sins because all sin was judged at Calvary.

Saints will be judged for their Works.

As a child of God, the saints will Bow to Him, Honor Him and Praise Him.

Heb 10:17	And their sins and iniquities will I remember no more.

This is the judgment of the believer's works, not the sins of the believer.

The sins of believers have been atoned for and are remembered no more.

II Tim 4:8	**8. Henceforth there is laid up for me a crown of righteousness, which the Lord, the righteous judge, shall give me at that day: and not to me only, but unto all them also that love his appearing.**

At the Judgment Seat of Christ, Rewards will be given to the faithful workers.

Rewards are earned by works. Saved by faith, Judged by works.

Every work will come into Judgment. Results is a gain of a reward or a loss of a reward.

Each child of God will be judged for their stewardship.

Some Saints will have greater rewards than others because they had greater faithfulness.

THE VIEW OF HEAVEN AFTER THE RAPTURE

To better understand the author's comments in this Book, please read the noted Verses of Revelation and then review the notes of the author.

Revelation 4

Read Rev. 4:1-11

Christ says to John, the writer of Revelation, "Come up here and I will show you things which must be hereafter."

John is placed into a realm of spiritual vision so he can see what Christ is telling him to write.

Seven lamps are burning before the Throne, which are the Seven Spirits of God.

The number 'seven' is God's number which denotes perfection.

Around God's Throne John sees four Heavenly Beasts, 24 Elders and the faithful souls from the old Testament and the Church age.

Each of the four Heavenly Beasts are full of eyes before and behind.

The first Beast is like a Lion.

The second Beast is like a Calf.

The third Beast has a face of a Man.

The fourth Beast is like a flying Eagle.

Each of the four Heavenly Beast have six wings and the wings are full of eyes before and behind.

The Heavenly Beast are saying,
"Holy, Holy, Holy, Lord God Almighty, which was, and is, and is to
come."

....

They are giving glory and honor and thanks to Him who sits on the
Throne and lives forever and ever.

....

Eternity is held by the Lord Jesus Christ.

....

THE LAMB WILL TAKE THE SEALS BOOK FROM GOD

Revelation 5

Read Rev. 5:1-14

John sees, in the right hand of God, a Book written and sealed with Seven Seals.

A mighty Angel is proclaiming, "Who is worthy to open the Book and loose the Seals?"

No man in Heaven nor in earth nor under the earth was able to open the Book or to even look upon it. No man is found worthy.

In the midst of the Throne stood a Lamb, (Christ), and He came and took the Book out of the right hand of God.

Christ proclaimed the Right and the Authority, by His death on the cross, to open the Book and loose the Seals.

The saints around the Throne are ten thousand times ten thousand and thousands and thousands. This is an innumerable number.

John sees an uncountable number of souls Praising God, Worshiping God, Glorifying God, Respecting God and being Reverence to God.

There is universal love, adoration and honor of the Lamb as King.

When Christ died on the cross it guaranteed the defeat of satan and his angels.

Christ's sacrifice also guaranties eternal results.

CHAPTER 8

BEGINNING OF THE SEVEN YEAR TRIBULATION

One second after the Rapture, God will remove all Godly influence on earth and allow wickedness to flourish. There will be no restrictions on evil.

The judgment of the world will be fully realized with the opening of the First Seal. God's wrath will be directed toward the wicked.

Just as death terminates the possibility of salvation for those who reject Christ today, so does the Rapture. Those who have heard the truth and rejected Christ prior to the Rapture, will not be able to be saved in the future because they have had their chance of salvation.

II Thess. 2:10-12

And with all deceivableness of unrighteousness in them that perish; because they received not the love of the truth, that they might be saved.

And for this cause God shall send them strong delusion, that they should believe a lie:

That they all might be damned who believed not the truth, but had pleasure in unrighteousness.

Because they rejected Christ when they had a chance to be saved, God will send them strong delusion.

Since they did not want the truth, God will have them believe the lies of the devil.

They will be damned because they believed not the Truth and had pleasure in unrighteousness.

....

God's wrath will come on the unsuspecting population of the world. The world will be caught unprepared for His punishments.

....

Once God's wrath begins, it will not end until it has accomplished its purpose.

....

FIRST THREE AND A HALF YEARS OF TRIBULATION

The Seven Seals Judgment

Revelation 6

Read Rev. 6:1-2   **Christ Opens the First Seal**

There will be a time span between the opening of each seal. How long a wait between each opening is not decided on earth but in Heaven.

The opening of the Seals will be after the Rapture.

It is not known how long it will be after the Rapture that Christ will open the First Seal. Is it Weeks, Months or Years? It is unknown.
Heaven will decide the Seal events that will be given to the earthly people.

The Final Judgment of earth is realized with the opening of the first seal.

John sees Christ open the first seal and reveal the antichrist of Falsehood.

Antichrist - the word itself means 'against Christ.'

Antichrist number one appears on a White horse.

WARNING: The first antichrist will come in the clouds riding a white horse to emulate the real true Christ. Do not be fooled as this is the beast of gross brutality and evil.

Antichrist number one will presents himself as a prince of peace and conquer.

He preaches peace yet prepares for war, brutality and dictatorship.

The antichrist is a conqueror and will deceive the people.

Read Rev. 6:3-4   **Christ Opens the Second Seal**

John sees Christ open the second seal and reveal the antichrist of War.

Antichrist number two appears on a Red horse.

He has the power of war and bloodshed.

He will be given a great sword.

He will take peace from the earth and the people will kill one another.

Read Rev. 6:5-6   **Christ Opens the Third Seal**

John sees Christ open the third seal and reveal the antichrist of Famine.

Antichrist number three appears on a Black horse.

He will take the world to the starvation level, creating massive famine and poverty on earth.

Famine usually comes after a war but this antichrist brings it with him.

The antichrist has a pair of balances in his hand which portrays that there will be a scarcity of food. Man nor the antichrist are allowed to harm the olive trees, which produces oil or the grape vines, which produces wine.

The world has rejected the Cross and the world faces judgment.

Read Rev. 6:7-8   **Christ Opens the Fourth Seal**

John sees Christ open the fourth seal and reveal the antichrist of Death.

Antichrist number four appears on a Pale horse.

The name of him that sits on the horse is Death.

The people of hell following after him.

He has the power to kill with the sword, hunger and death.

He will distribute a high degree of suffering and pain.

There will be numerous antichrists and false prophets and they will deceive many.

....

Many people will die and many will go directly to hell.

....

This ends the first three and a half years of the Seven Year Tribulation period.

....

LAST THREE AND A HALF YEARS OF GREAT TRIBULATION

There will be a time span between the opening of each seal. How long a wait between each opening is not decided on earth but in Heaven.

Read Rev. 6:9-11 **Christ Opens the Fifth Seal**

Christ open the fifth seal and reveal the cries of Martyrs. (Saints and Godly People).

John hears the cries of the Saints from under the Altar.

John sees the souls of them on earth that are slain because they believe the Word of God.

These are saints that are saved after the Rapture who never heard the plan of salvation prior to the Rapture.

God will not forget or forsake these redeemed souls.

White robes are given to each of them. The white robes symbolizes righteousness of the saints.

The Martyrs must remain on earth until the end of the seven year Tribulation. All people that were saved during this period will be delivered unto Heaven.

Isa. 34:4-6   And all the host of heaven shall be dissolved, and the heavens shall be rolled together as a scroll: and all their host shall fall down, as the leaf falleth off from the vine, and as a falling fig from the fig tree.

For my sword shall be bathed in heaven: behold, it shall come down upon Idumea, and upon the people of my curse, to judgment.

The sword of the LORD is filled with blood, it is made fat with fatness, and with the blood of

lambs and goats, with the fat of the kidneys of rams: for the LORD hath a sacrifice in Bozrah, and a great slaughter in the land of Idumea.

Read Rev. 6:12-17 **Christ Opens the Sixth Seal**

God is preparing to do major surgery on the earth itself and to carry the slaughter of evil all the way to Armageddon.

John sees Christ open the sixth seal and reveal the antichrist of anarchy, confusion, turmoil and lawlessness.

There is great cosmic disturbances, rearrangements and reorganizations of earth and heavenly properties.

There is a great earthquake.

The sun becomes black.

The moon becomes as blood.

Stars fall from Heaven to earth (meteorites).

There will be such a bombardment on the earth by the meteorites that the earth will sustain great damage.

There are mighty winds and great storms.

Heaven departs and rolls back as a scroll and every Mountain and every Island shakes and are moved out of their locations.

The Sixth Seal shows unimaginable proportions of power for:
> *Every king of the earth.*
> *Every great man.*
> *Every rich man.*
> *Every chief captain.*
> *Every mighty man.*
> *Every bondman.*
> *Every free man will hide themselves in the mountains and rocks.*

Mankind will beg the mountains to hide them from the face of God and from the wrath of the Lamb (Christ).

Everyone will try to hide themselves from God, from the poverty level to the richest of the land.

Mankind cannot hide from God.

Mankind will seek death but will not find it.

Mankind has set themselves against God ever since the fall of Adam and Eve.

As the Seals are opened, Mankind will see how powerful God really is.

THE PEOPLE OF ISRAEL ARE SEALED, 144,000 SOULS

Revelation 7

Read Rev. 7:1-8

Christ will delay the opening of the Seventh Seal for a short period of time to address the people of Israel and the Tribulation saints.

John sees four angels standing at the four corners of the earth, holding back the judgments from harming the earth until Israel is sealed.

Israel's sealed salvation is a promise of God through Jesus Christ.

John hears the number of Jews that are sealed. The number is one hundred and forty-four thousand of all the tribes of the children of Israel.

Twelve Tribes, twelve thousand from each tribe:
> *Tribe of Judah.*
> *Tribe of Reuben.*
> *Tribe of Gad.*
> *Tribe of Aser.*

> *Tribe of Nephthalim.*
> *Tribe of Manasses.*
> *Tribe of Simeon.*
> *Tribe of Levi.*

> *Tribe of Issachar.*
> *Tribe of Zabulon.*
> *Tribe of Joseph.*
> *Tribe of Benjamin.*

The one hundred and forty-four thousand are preserved by God and cannot be killed by anyone.

They will become preachers and evangelists to the Tribulation people and many people will be saved.

The Church is removed from earth at the time of the Rapture, which is prior to the beginning of the Tribulation period.

THE TRIBULATION SAINTS

Read Rev. 7:9-17

John sees a great multitude of Gentiles which no man can count of all nations, tribes, peoples and tongues, standing before the Throne and before the Lamb.

These are the saints who were saved during the seven year Tribulation.

They shall never hunger nor thirst anymore; the sun will not strike them, nor any heat.

God will wipe away the tears from their eyes.

Both Jews and Gentiles will be saved during the Tribulation period.

God has brought about salvation by what Christ did at the Cross.

Christ gave Himself in Sacrifice at the Cross by atoning for all sin.

The Saints have robes as white as snow because they had washed them in the blood of the Lamb.

They will be saved on the same basis as those before the Tribulation. Saved by faith, in the life of Jesus, in the death of Jesus and in the resurrection of Jesus.

Revelation 8

Read Rev. 8:1　　　***Christ Opens the Seventh Seal***

The Seventh Seal will produce much Judgment.

John sees Christ open the seventh seal and it breaks the hearts of the Heavenly Host.

There is Silence in Heaven for about half an hour.

The Silence is deafening and overpowering.

One second ago Heaven was talking, praising, celebrating, worshiping and rejoicing, now there is complete silence.

There is nothing that has ever happened on earth that silenced Heaven.

Adam and Eve's sin, did not silence Heaven.

The great flood that killed all mankind except Noah's family, did not silence Heaven.

Christ's death on the Cross, did not silence Heaven.

The opening of the first six seals, will not silence Heaven.

The beginning of the Tribulation Period, will not silence Heaven.

But the opening of the Seventh Seal, will silence Heaven.

It is the absolute reality of the end of salvation opportunities.

The opening of the seventh seal slams the door to the deliverance from sin.

No more open door to Heaven.

No more opportunities to be saved.

God is so grieved by the sins of mankind that there is a Holy stillness in Heaven.

God stops all Heavenly activities.

God's heart is heavy because He does not want anyone to go to hell.

Even the Heavenly Saints are offering prayers at the Altar of God, praying that the lost people will repent.

The Silence declares the dramatic doom and the intensity of judgment that is coming upon mankind.

The first Six Seals are a demonstration of God's disappointment and frustration with man.

The Seventh Seal of the Seal-Judgments will bring great destruction.

....

The Seventh Seal is the prelude to the Seven Trumpets and the Seven Vials of Judgment upon the earth.

....

Mankind will go through these judgments with horror and sorrow, and still be faced with eternity in an everlasting hell.

....

These Judgments are not symbolic events, they are Literal.

....

Luke 21:25-28

25 And there shall be signs in the sun, and in the moon, and in the stars; and upon the earth distress of nations, with perplexity; the sea and the waves roaring;

26 Men's hearts failing them for fear, and for looking after those things which are coming on the earth: for the powers of heaven shall be shaken.

27 And then shall they see the Son of man coming in a cloud with power and great glory.

28 And when these things begin to come to pass, then look up, and lift up your heads; for your redemption draweth nigh.

THE SEVEN TRUMPET JUDGMENTS

Read Rev. 8:2-6

John sees Seven Angels stand before God and are given Seven Trumpets.

Another Angel takes the Censer (a vessel that holds Incense) and fills it with fire from the Altar of God and throws it to earth.

The Censer causes noises, thundering, lightning and earthquakes.

The earth will undergo hardships and difficulties such as the world has never seen.

Read Rev. 8:7   **The First Angel sounds the First Trumpet.**

Hail and fire mingled with blood is cast upon the earth.

One-third of the trees are reduced to ashes.

All green grass is totally burned.

Breathing is difficult. The air is full of ash, soot, embers and deadly heat.

Read Rev. 8:8-9   **The Second Angel sounds the Second Trumpet.**

A great fire-burning mountain is cast into the sea. Most likely it is a large Meteorite.

One-third of the sea becomes blood.

One-third of the creatures in the sea die.

One-third of the ships on the sea are destroyed.

The rot and strong odor of the dead humans and sea creatures, produces a stench that is intolerable, extreme and beyond endurance.

Read Rev. 8:10-11   **The Third Angel sounds the Third Trumpet.**

A great star falls from Heaven burning as a meteorite.

The name of the star is Wormwood.

The meteorite falls on one-third of the rivers.

It also falls on one-third of the drinking water.

The water becomes bitter because Wormwood in the water causes Pain, Suffering, Distress and Agony.

Thousands die from drinking the poisonous water.

Read Rev. 8:12-13   ***The Fourth Angel sounds the Fourth Trumpet.***

One-third of the Sun is darkened.

One-third of the Moon is darkened.

One-third of the Stars are darkened.

One-third of the Day will not shine.

One-third of the Night will not appear.

These Judgments are not symbolic events, they are Literal.

CHAPTER 9

DEMON LOCUSTS TORMENTS MANKIND

Revelation 9

Read Rev. 9:1-12 ***The Fifth Angel sounds the Fifth Trumpet.***

A Star will fall from Heaven.

To him is given the key to the bottomless pit. The one receiving the key in satan himself.

Satan opens the bottomless pit.

The bottomless pit is hell itself.

The pit releases smoke and heat as from a great furnace.

The sun and the air are darkened by the smoke.

Demon locusts with stingers in their tails come out of the pit. .

The locusts are as large as horses with:
> *The face of a man.*
> *The hair of a woman.*
> *The teeth of a lion.*
> *The tail of a scorpion.*
> *The wings of an eagle.*

The demon locusts are not allowed to hurt the grass, the trees or anything that is green.

There will be saints on earth at this time, those that are saved during the Tribulation and the 144,000 Jews. The locusts are not allowed to hurt the saints sealed by God.

They can only attack the unsaved.

The locusts are to sting and torment sinful man for five months but not to kill them.

Man will suffer and receive great pain during this period.

Man will seek death but will not find it. They will desire to die but death will flee from them.

Man cannot even commit suicide.

The fallen angel of the bottomless pit commands the locusts.

The fallen angel's Greek name is Apollyon.

Apollyon is the angel who threw in with the devil Lucifer in the Rebellion against God. His name means destroyer.

There are only four angels named in the Bible.

Gabriel and Michael, both Heavenly Righteous Angels.

Lucifer and Apollyon, both powerful fallen angels. Although they are powerful, they can only perform punishments that God allows them to do.

Read Rev. 9:13-21 **The Sixth Angel sounds the Sixth Trumpet.**

John hears a voice from the Altar of Heaven saying to the sixth Angel, "Loose the four angels which are bound in the river Euphrates."

These angels are evil angels but God will use them for His Will.

The four evil angels are released and God prepares them to execute His wrath on mankind.

John sees the demon army which numbered two hundred thousand thousand which calculates to be an army of 200 million.

God will use this army to execute His sixth Trumpet plague on man.

These are demon spirits riding demon horses.

The heads of the horses are as heads of lions.

Out of the mouth of the horses comes fire, smoke and brimstone.

One-third of mankind is killed by the fire, smoke and brimstone.

Those still living refuse to repent of their sins and give up their worship of devils and idols.

They refuse to give up their Murdering, Sorceries, Fornications and Thefts.

An Angel with a Little Opened Book

*** *** *** *** ***

Revelation 10

*** *** *** *** ***

Read Rev. 10:1-7

*** *** *** *** ***

John sees a Mighty Angel come down from Heaven.

*** *** *** *** ***

He is clothed with a cloud and a rainbow on his head.

*** *** *** *** ***

He has a face as the sun and his feet are as pillows of fire.

*** *** *** *** ***

He has a little Book open in his hand.

*** *** *** *** ***

He sets his right foot upon the sea and his left foot on the land.

*** *** *** *** ***

The Angel cries out and the Seven Thunders speak.

*** *** *** *** ***

John is told from Heaven, "Do not write what the Seven Thunders say."

*** *** *** *** ***

There is no record of what was said by the seven Thunders.

*** *** *** *** ***

John sees the Angel which stands upon the sea and upon the earth, lift up His hands to Heaven and speaks to:
> *Him who lives forever and ever.*
> *Him who created Heaven.*
> *Him who created earth.*
> *Him who created the things that are.*
> *Him who created the sea.*
> *Him who created the things which are within.*

*** *** *** *** ***

The world belongs to God by virtue and worthiness of Him being the Creator.

*** *** *** *** ***

John Eats the Little Book

Read Rev. 10:8-11

Heaven speaks to John saying,
  "Go and take the little open Book which is held by the
  Angel that stands upon the sea and upon land."

John took the little Book from the Angel.

The Angel told John to eat it.

John ate the little book.

The Book is Sweet as honey in the mouth but Bitter in the belly.

The little Book contains Sweetness:
  The Sweetness of the Word Of God.
  The Sweetness of the Love From God.
  The Sweetness of the Salvation By God.
  The Sweetness of Heaven With God.

The little Book contains Bitterness:
  The Bitterness of the Wrath Of God.
  The Bitterness of the Sadness From God.
  The Bitterness of the Judgment By God.
  The Bitterness of Hell Without God.

Sin seems sweet while living it but becomes bitter while trying to digest it.

GOD'S TWO WITNESSES ON EARTH DURING THE GREAT TRIBULATION

Revelation 11

Read Rev. 11:1-6

During the last three and a half years of the Great Tribulation period, God will have two witnesses on earth that will prophesy and preach repentance.

The identity of the two witnesses is not revealed in the Bible.

However, there were two men in the Bible that never saw earthly death.

Enoch is one of two men in history who did not die an earthly death, the other is Elijah.

Gen. 5:24   **And Enoch walked with God: and he was not; for God took him.**

Hebrews 11:5   **By faith Enoch was translated that he should not see death: And was not found, because God had translated him: for before his translation he had this testimony, that he pleased God.**

2 Kings 2:11   **And it came to pass, as they still went on, and talked, that, behold, there appeared a chariot of fire, and horses of fire, and parted them both asunder; and Elijah went up by a whirlwind into heaven.**

God took these two men to heaven to be with Him.

God may allow them to come back to earth to preach to the lost.

There is no Bible proof that the two men are Enoch and Elijah.

God's two witnesses will have the power to devour their enemies by fire from their mouths. The fire will be toward their enemies and this is their punishment.

They will have the force to stop the rain from Heaven but let it rain when they want.

They will have the authority to turn water to blood.

They will have the ability to punish the earth with plagues. Plagues of sicknesses and diseases. Plagues of insects such as frogs, flies, ants, roaches and such.

Their ministry is forty-two months; they cannot be harmed during this period.

The Two Witnesses Killed

Read Rev. 11:7-10

At the end of the forty-two months of exposing the wickedness of mankind, the antichrist from the bottomless pit will make war against the two witnesses and kill them.

The world will rejoice and celebrate the death of the two witnesses.

The two bodies will lie in the street for three and a half days.

The enemies of the two witnesses will not allow the bodies to be put into the ground.

The Two Witnesses Resurrected

Read Rev. 11:10-13

The Spirit of God will resurrect the two witnesses and they will stand up.

God will say to the two witnesses, "Come up hither."

They will immediately ascend into Heaven and their enemies will watch them as they go upward.

Great fear will fall upon the people of hate.

This is the Last Day of the seven year Tribulation.

The people on earth at this time are:
The Saved Jews.
The Saved Gentiles.
The antichrists.
The unsaved.

God will send an earthquake within the hour.

One-tenth of the city will be destroyed.

Seven thousand people will die.

The Kingdom Proclaimed

Read Rev. 11:14-19 **The Seventh Angel sounds the Seventh Trumpet.**

Loud voices in Heaven will proclaim the kingdoms of the world as the kingdoms of our Lord.

The Heavenly saints will fall upon their knees and worship the Lord God Almighty.

The nations will be angered and it will lead to Armageddon.

The temple of God is opened and the Ark of the Covenant is there. Heaven displays voices, thundering, lightning, earthquakes and great hail.

The Great White Throne Judgment for Non-Christians will be coming soon.

God directed John to write these chapters,
To Inform mankind.
To Advise mankind.
To Educate mankind.
To Notify mankind.
To Warn mankind of things that are ahead.

NOTE:

Some of the recorded events in the book of Revelation happened in the past, others will happen in the future. These are things that will happen at the end of time, but not necessarily in the order that God allowed John to see, to hear and to write down.

Starting with Chapter 12, some of the events, in some of the chapters, are not in chronological sequence with other happenings in the Book of Revelation.

Chapter 12 reminds mankind of the position that Israel holds within God's eternal plan. Some of these happenings occurred many years ago and some will occur when God says they will.

John Sees into the Past

Revelation 12

Read Rev. 12:1-6   ***The Woman, the Child, and the Dragon***

There appears a great sign in Heaven, a woman clothed with the sun, and the moon is under her feet and upon her head a crown of twelve stars. She is with child.

There appears another sign in Heaven, a red dragon.

The woman gives birth to a boy child, who is one day to rule the nations.

The boy child is caught up to God and His throne in Heaven.

Satan, the red dragon, having seven heads, represents the countries that persecuted Israel.

The woman is Israel.
The child is Christ.
The red dragon is satan.

Mid-point of the seven year tribulation, the antichrist will turn on Israel. He will demand the people worship him.

The woman will flee into the wilderness. The woman is Israel.

The people of Israel will go to another country, a country which God has prepared for them.

They will stay there until the tribulation period is over.

Satan wants to be bigger than God, better than God and higher than God. Satan has an ego and pride problem and wants heaven to bow down to him.

Satan is thrown out of Heaven

Read Rev. 12:7-9

John sees a war in Heaven, Archangel Michael and the Heavenly Angels are fighting against the dragon and his angels. Michael is a Chief Angel, a High Ranking Angel in Heaven.

The dragon and his angels do not prevail in the battle; neither was their place found any more in Heaven.

The great dragon was cast out of Heaven into the earth along with the angels that sided with him.

Jude 1:6   **And the angels which kept not their first estate, but left their own habitation, he hath reserved in everlasting chains under darkness unto the judgment of the great day.**

These evil angels were banished from Heaven and were placed in chains and darkness.

They will remain there until the Great White Throne Judgment, then they will be put into the Lake of Fire that burns forever and ever.

God threw them out of Heaven, one day God will throw them out of earth and into hell.

Read Rev. 12:10-17

John hears loud voices in Heaven saying, "Now is come Salvation, and Strength, and the Kingdom of our God and the power of His Christ, for the accuser of our brethren is cast down."

Woe to the people of earth for the devil is come down unto them having great wrath and anger.

The devil knows he has a short time to carry out his plan.

He finds himself on earth with his army of evil angels. With his army he will attack Israel.

God will step in and care for and protect Israel for three and a half years.

The devil will cast out a flood toward Israel. Is it a flood of real water or a flood of evil angels? It doesn't really matter because God opens up the earth and swallows up the flood.

The devil begins to attack everyone who keeps God's commandments and he will continue until judgment day.

Satan is the master of deception and the prince of darkness.

He only has power in these two areas.

Christ will rule this World, not satan.

Chapter 13 is inserted into the Book of Revelation to speak of things that are coming to the people on earth. God will enforce His plan of judgment against mankind within His timeframe.

THE BEAST AND THE FALSE PROPHET

Revelation 13

Read Rev. 13: 1-10 **The Rise and Rule of the Beast and False Prophet**

John sees a beast rise up out of the sea, having seven heads and ten horns, and upon his horns, ten crowns and upon his seven heads the name of blasphemy, each defying and insulting God.

The beast opens his mouth and blasphemes God's name, God's Tabernacle and God's Heavenly Host.

Blasphemy is the strongest word or writing or action that mocks, ridicules or makes fun of God or anything Devine.

The fallen angel (satan) and the antichrist are the beasts.

The beasts looked like a leopard with feet of a bear and a mouth of a lion.

Satan gives the antichrist great power and authority to spread evil throughout the world.

The sinful world will worship the beast and follow him. .

The antichrist breaks the covenant with Israel.

He comes to the Jewish Temple and demands that he be worshiped as God.

The antichrist will maintain power over the people for three and a half years of the Great Tribulation.

More of the world turns to worshiping the beast as he demonstrates superhuman ability.

John sees another beast rise up out of the earth with a Lamb-like appearance to deceive the people.

This antichrist will claim to be Christ and people will worship the evil beast.

If any man has an ear let him hear. Those who will not hear the Word of God but hear the word of the antichrist, will receive the worst type of bondage.

The second coming of Christ will bring swift Judgment upon the followers of the antichrist.

Israel and the ten nations will be ruled and controlled by the antichrist.

Those with their names written in the Book of Life will not worship the antichrist.

The Book of Life is the Heaven Reservation Book that is maintained by God for those that believe in Jesus Christ. The reservation is for eternal life in Heaven with God.

Unbelievers names are not found in the Lamb's Book of Life.

Read Rev. 13:11-18 **The Beast with a number of a man, 666**

Another beast comes up out of the earth.

The false prophet makes fire come down from Heaven to earth in the sight of men.

The antichrist will actually bring the fire down through the power of satan.

The beast will deceive mankind by his means of miracles.

The beast is given great power by satan and he demonstrates that power.

The antichrist tells the people to make an image of the beast.

The antichrist gives the image of the beast a spirit and the ability to speak.

The image of the beast tells the people to worship the image.

All the world marveled and followed the beast.

Those that do not worship the image of the beast will be killed by being beheaded.

The antichrist demands that mankind have the mark of the beast on their right hand or on their forehead, or the name of the beast, to be able to buy or sell.

The mark of the beast number is 666. Man was created on the sixth day, so this is a number of a man, not of God.

The number six represents evil. Six, six, six, (666) is evil multiplied over and over.

Chapter 14 is a chapter that is placed at this particular point in Revelation for the information that it contains. The actual happenings will be at another time.

THE LAMB AND THE ISRAEL SAINTS

Revelation 14

Read Rev. 14:1-7   ***The Lamb and the 144,000 Jews***

Christ is referred to as a 'Lamb' and referenced 28 times in the Book of Revelation.

John sees Christ the Lamb, standing on Mount Sion with the one hundred and forty-four thousand Jews that were saved during the first half of the Great Tribulation period. The Jews have His Father's name written on their foreheads.

They are singing a new song before the Throne of God.

A song that God reserved for the saints of Israel. No one else can learn this song.

John sees another Angel flying in Heaven, having the everlasting Gospel to preach unto them who dwell on earth.

The Angel has an urgency to preach to every nation, and kindred, and tongue, and people.

The Angel will describe the Life, Death and Resurrection of Jesus Christ and he will plead with mankind to repent of their sins.

The Angel will be observed and heard over the entire earth. God will allow all of mankind to see and hear the Angel.

The Angel's voice is saying, "Fear God, and give Glory to Him, for the hour of Judgment is come and worship Him who made Heaven and Earth."

God continues to provide man with a way to Salvation.

BABYLON'S FALL FORETOLD

Read Rev. 14:8-13

The word Babylon is used in the Book of Revelation and refers to an evil and persecuting system that will be destroyed by God for its wickedness. It is a one world order of spiritual adultery, corruption and anti-Christian.

An Angel tells the world that Babylon has fallen because of her rebellion and wickedness.

A third Angel appears with a warning:

Warning 1.   *If any man worships the beast and his image and receives the mark of the beast, then he will drink of the wine of the wrath of God without mercy and he will be tormented with fire and brimstone in the eternal hell.*

Warning 2.   *Mankind will be judged in the presence of the Holy Angels and in the presence of the Lamb at the Great White Throne Judgment.*

Warning 3.	*Smoke of the torment will ascend upward forever and ever as the conscious man lives in his own choosing.*
Warning 4.	*There will be no rest day or night, the agony will be an unbroken continuance of misery.*
Warning 5.	*Those that chose to take the mark of the beast condemns themselves to hell because they have chosen the devil-way over the Christ-way.*
Warning 6.	*Taking the mark of the beast is blaspheming the Holy Spirit, for which there is no forgiveness.*
Warning 7.	*This is the sin unto death, the unpardonable sin. This is the sin of rejection and is defined as blasphemy against the Holy Spirit.*
Warning 8.	*The mark of the beast is spiritual death.*

John hears a voice from Heaven telling him to write, "Blessed are they who die in the Lord for they shall have rest from their labor and their works will follow them."

JOHN SEES, A VISION OF THE ARMAGEDDON BATTLE

Read Rev. 14:14-20

John sees a white cloud and on the cloud is one that looks to be the Son of Man, Jesus Christ Himself.

On His head is a golden crown and in His hand is a sharp sickle. (A sickle is a hand-held tool with a long curved blade which may be used to harvest grain.)

Angel One comes out of the Temple, crying with a loud voice, to Him that sits on the cloud, "Thrust in your sickle and reap for the harvest of the earth is ripe."

He who sits on the cloud thrust His sickle onto the earth and the earth is reaped.

Reaping the Grapes of Wrath

Angel Two comes out of the Temple and he also has a sharp sickle.

Angle Three comes out from the Altar and he has the power over fire.

Angel Three cries to Him with the sharp sickle to reap the vines of the earth.

The Angel thrusted his sickle into the earth and gathered the vines and threw them into the winepress.

John sees the flow of blood from the battle of good and evil. It runs out of the winepress into a valley.

The battle produces a flow of blood about six feet deep and about two hundred miles long.

Chapter 15 is for guidance and direction for things that will happen later. It is an introduction to the vial judgments.

THE SEVEN VIALS JUDGMENTS

Revelation 15

Read Rev. 15:1-8 **The Vial Judgment Angels get their Plague Assignments**

John sees the seven Angels in Heaven that will be given the plague assignments for earth.

This is the concluding judgments of the antichrist, which will be the worst judgments of all.

These judgments will show the displeased wrath of God.

John sees, standing before the Throne of God, the saints that will get victory over the beast (antichrist).

These are the saints that refused to take the mark of the beast and will be killed by the antichrist during the Tribulation.

The saints are singing the song of Moses and the song of the Lamb in worship.

This is the song that Moses wrote and taught to the people.

John sees the temple of the tabernacle in Heaven and it is open.

One of the four heavenly beast gives the seven Angels seven golden vials full of the wrath of God.

Out of the temple comes the seven Angels with the seven plagues of the vial judgments.

The temple is filled with smoke from the Glory of God and His power.

No one is to enter the temple until the seven plagues are fulfilled.

These vials will be the worst judgments yet. They are filled with the wrath of God, without mercy.

These judgments will take place near the end of the Great Tribulation.

Chapter 16 is the delivery of the seven vials of judgments. The Vial events will come near the end of the seven year tribulation.

THE SEVEN VIALS OF THE WRATH OF GOD

Revelation 16

Read Rev. 16:1-12
John hears a great voice out of the temple telling the seven Angels to go and pour out the vials of the Wrath of God upon the kingdoms of the antichrist.

The first Angel pouring out his vial upon the earth.

Offensive and dreadful sores and boils appears upon the men that have the mark of the beast, and upon them which worshipped the beast image.

The second Angel pours out his vial upon the sea.

The sea becomes as blood of a dead man and every living creature in the sea dies.

The third Angel pours out his vial upon the rivers and fountains.

All waters become blood. The rivers, the fountains, the waterfalls, the lakes, the ponds, the dams and every puddle of water in the land is now blood.

John hears the Angel of the waters say, "Thou art righteous, O Lord and hast judged thus for they have shed the blood of saints and prophets, and thou hast given them blood to drink."

Many saints suffered and were murdered by the antichrist.

The fourth Angel pours out his vial upon the sun.

The Angel scorches the men with great fire and heat.

The sun will pour out more heat on the earth than any time in existence.

Mankind already have boils on their bodies and a water shortage, yet they respond by cursing and blaspheming the name of God rather than repent.

The fifth Angel pours out his vial upon the seat of the beast and the headquarters of the antichrist.

The antichrist kingdom becomes full of darkness.

Men gnaw their tongues because of their great pain from their boils.

The heart of mankind is so corrupt and evil that even these judgments will not change their attitude and spirit.

Man continues to blaspheme God and repent not of their deeds.

The sixth Angel pours out his vial upon the river of Euphrates.

The water of the great river Euphrates dries up and becomes dust. God needs this land dry in preparation for the Battle of Armageddon.

Read Rev 16:13-16

John sees three unclean spirits like frogs.

The spirits come:
    Out of the mouth of the dragon.
    Out of the mouth of the beast.
    Out of the mouth of the false prophet.

They are the spirits of devils working miracles on earth to influence the kingdoms of the world to join their army against God at Armageddon.

Armageddon is a literal place where a literal battle will be fought.

Millions will die at the Battle of Armageddon.

The seventh Angel pours out his vial into the air

Read Rev. 16:17-21

This is the last of the Tribulation Judgments from God.

There came a voice from the Throne of Heaven saying, "It is done."

The last time such words were echoed, "It is finished", we heard it from the Cross when Christ said, "It is finished" and then He died for the sins of the world.

This earthquake mightier than anything man and this world has ever seen.

Cities are divided and nations are destroyed.

Every island sinks and every mountain disappears. Mountains become as pebbles on the sand. The mountains and the islands cannot be found.

Heaven rains down great hail. Each hailstone weighing about one hundred pounds.

Sinful man continue to blaspheme God.

The plagues are exceedingly great and mankind is helpless against God, yet they repent not.

Chapter 17 is another chapter that is not in chronological sequence with other events in Revelation. This chapter describes the evil in the world and how the devils, antichrists and satan tricks people into thinking that the one world religion is the correct way to eternal happiness.

THE DOOM OF BABYLON

Revelation 17

John sees The Scarlet Woman and the Scarlet Beast

Read Rev. 17:1-18

One of the seven Angels which had delivered one of the vials of wrath upon the earth speaks to John.

The Angel says,
"Come John and I will show you the judgment of the great whore who sits upon many waters and many people."

(The word 'whore' is referring to all the false religions of the world which were devised by man as a substitute for Jesus Christ and Him crucified.)

The Angel shows John:
>*The beauty of the whore.*
>*The beauty of her clothes.*
>*The beauty of her gold.*
>*The beauty of all her fine things.*

These things influence sinful man to enjoy the scarlets of the world.

The whore is the mother of harlots. She is drunk with the blood of the saints and the martyrs.

The antichrist tells the people that these pleasures come with the one world religion, so enjoy yourself.

The people are willing to trust the beast.

The evil in man draws man to the false religions.

This is the highest level of deception by satan.

The nations gives their power to the beast.

The beast will make war with the Lamb and the Lamb will overcome because He is Lord of lords and King of kings.

....

The antichrist will kill the great whore, which are the world false religions. He will wipe them out. These religions will be replaced by 'beast worship'.

....

BABYLON IS DESTROYED

Revelation 18

John sees The Fall of Babylon the Great

Read Rev. 18:1-8

Another Angel comes down from Heaven with great power.

The earth is lightened by the glory of the Angel.

The Angel announces, "Babylon the great is fallen, is fallen."

Babylon is full of demons, devils, spirits and false prophets.

John hears another voice from Heaven saying, "My people, come out of Babylon or receive her plagues, for her sins have reached Heaven and God remembers."

God says,
> *"Judgment has come to Babylon and there will be much torment and sorrow."*

Evil says to God,
> *"We are queen of the universe and we are stronger than you."*

God says,
> *"I will destroy you in one day with fire, earthquakes and death."*

God will demonstrate His power to the world.

The World Mourns Babylon's Destruction

....

Read Rev. 18:9-24

....

The kings of the earth, shipmasters and sailors watch as their worldly goods are burned to the ground.

....

God destroys Babylon in one hour.

....

A mighty Angel takes a great millstone and casts it into the sea saying, "That great city of Babylon shall be found no more."

....

Neither will there be music or craftsmen or millstones turning or lights or marriage or witchcraft found any more.

....

Those that choose the mark of the beast, are choosing hell for eternity.

....

The fall of Babylon clears the way for the primary theme of Revelation, the second coming of Christ and the establishment of the Kingdom of God.

....

JOHN SEES HEAVEN'S WIN OVER BABYLON

Revelation 19

Read Rev. 19:1-10

John hears many great voices in Heaven singing praises unto God and His salvation, for salvation is God and belongs to God.

God will finish the judgment of the false religions in the world and will avenge the blood of the saints.

Babylon will be destroyed and her smoke will rise up forever and ever because her judgment is eternal.

The twenty-four elders and the four beasts in Heaven fall down and worship God.

A voice comes out of the Throne saying,
> *"Everyone, small and great, praise God forever and ever."*

John hears other voices, voices of great multitude and as mighty thunders. These are the voices of the believers in Heaven and they are praising the Lord God who reigns.

The Heavenly body of believers will be at the marriage of the Lamb. The wife will be the redeemed saints of all generations.

Another voice tells John to write,
> *"Blessed are they which are called unto the marriage supper of the Lamb."*

As this voice speaks, John can see it is a man. John falls down to worship him.

The man tells John not to worship him because he is a fellow servant and brethren.

CHAPTER 10

THE SECOND COMING OF CHRIST

At the end of the seven year Tribulation, Christ returns to earth to rule, to reign and to judge the world.

Read Rev. 19:11-14

Heaven opens and beholds a white horse.

He who sits upon the horse is called Faithful to His Promise to Return and True to come in Judgment.

In righteousness He does judge and make war as He said He would do at His second coming.

His eyes are as a flame of fire.

On His head are many crowns.

He has a name written that no man knows but He himself. It is unknown to man.

He is clothed with a vesture dipped in blood, His own blood.

His name is called The Word of God.

His army, which are the Saints of Heaven, are following Him on their white horses, clothed in white linen.

Every saint of God who ever lived will come with Christ at the second coming. Everyone on earth will see Christ when He returns to earth.

....

When Christ comes at the Rapture, only Christians can see Him.

....

Non-Christians cannot see Christ in the clouds at the Rapture.

....

THE BATTLE AT ARMAGEDDON

....

Read Rev. 19:15-16

....

John sees Christ and out of His mouth comes a sharp sword. With it He will smite all the nations that joined the antichrist and He is ready for battle.

....

Christ will rule with a rod of iron.

....

To erase any doubt of who He is, Christ has written on His vesture and on His thigh, KING OF KINGS, AND LORD OF LORDS

....

Read Rev. 19:17-19

....

John sees an Angel saying to the fowls in the sky,
"Come and get supper which is supplied by God. You can eat:
>*The flesh of Kings.*
>*The flesh of Captains.*
>*The flesh of Mighty Men.*
>*The flesh of Horses.*
>*The flesh of the Riders.*
>*The flesh of all Men, Free and Bond, Small and Great"*

....

John sees the antichrist and the earthly kings with their armies and they number about two hundred million.

....

They are gathered together to make war against Christ and His Heavenly Army.

....

Armageddon will be a battle between the forces of good and evil.

....

The battle will take place in the hill country surrounding the plains of Megiddo, about sixty miles north of Jerusalem.

....

This location has a plain where many battles have taken place over the centuries.

....

The antichrist will lead the armies of the nations and the world into battle.

....

The evil armies will come from everywhere, the north, the south, the east and the west.

THE DOOM OF THE BEAST AND THE FALSE PROPHET

Read Rev. 19:20-21

Christ takes the beast and the false prophet and casts them both alive into the Lake of Fire and Brimstone.

The rest of the armies are slain with the sword of Him who sat on the white horse.

Christ will speak the Word at the Armageddon battle and whatever He speaks will take place.

The slain will lie where they fall.

The dead will not be buried, their bodies will be left for the birds and vultures.

The vultures will be filled with the flesh of every earthly thing killed during the battle.

SATAN IS BOUND AND PLACED IN THE BOTTOMLESS PIT

Revelation 20

Satan Bound for One Thousand Years

Read Rev. 20:1-3

John sees an Angel come down from Heaven with the key to the bottomless pit and a great chain in his hand.

The Angel puts his hands on satan and binds him with the chain for a thousand years.

The Heavenly Angel casts him who he chained into the bottomless pit.

He then locks him up, and sets a seal upon him.

Satan is locked away so he cannot deceive the nations.

He will remain in hell for one thousand years.

At the end of the thousand years, satan will be released for a little season.

Satan will again deceive the nations.

BEGINNING OF THE MILLENNIUM, 1000 YEARS OF PEACE

Read Rev. 20:4-6

John sees Thrones, and those that sit upon the Thrones, and judgment was given unto them.

John sees the souls of those that were beheaded during the Tribulation period:
> *For their witness of Jesus.*
> *For the Word of the Lord.*
> *For not worshipping the beast.*
> *For not worshipping the image.*
> *For not taking the mark of the beast.*
> *And they lived and reigned with Christ a thousand years.*

The rest of the dead, the unsaved, live not again until the thousand years are finished.

There are two resurrections. The resurrection of the Just and the resurrection of the Unjust.

The saints will be with Christ and have no fear of the second death.

The unsaved people that have died since the dawn of time will remain body dead.

The souls and spirits of the unsaved have lived in hell since their physical death.

The resurrection of the unsaved will come after the thousand year reign. This is the second resurrection.

The first resurrection is the Rapture Resurrection of the saved souls.

The second death will be the unsaved souls being cast into the Lake of Fire and be there forever and ever.

Isaiah 11:6-8	**From the sole of the foot even unto the head there is no soundness in it; but wounds, and bruises, and putrifying sores: they have not been closed, neither bound up, neither mollified with ointment.**
	Your country is desolate, your cities are burned with fire: your land, strangers devour it in your presence, and it is desolate, as overthrown by strangers.
	And the daughter of Zion is left as a cottage in a vineyard, as a lodge in a garden of cucumbers, as a besieged city.

During the Millennium, the nature of the animal world will be totally changed.

The wolf and lamb will eat together.

The leopard and kid (baby goat) will eat together.

The cow and bear will eat together.

The lion and the ox will eat together.

AT THE END OF THE THOUSAND YEARS

Read Rev. 20:7-9

When the thousand years are finished, satan will be loose out of his prison.

Satan will go out to deceive the nations again. God will allow this to happen because it is within His plan..

Satan will locate the people that have never accepted Christ as their Savior.

Satan will gather them for battle.

Satan's army will be as sand of the sea, a number that is not countable.

Satan and his armies will come to fight God and Jerusalem. This will be satan's last stand.

Jesus took the Armageddon battle, God Himself will take this one.

Zech 14:12-13   **And this shall be the plague wherewith the LORD will smite all the people that have fought against Jerusalem; Their flesh shall consume away while they stand upon their feet, and their eyes shall consume away in their holes, and their tongue shall consume away in their mouth.**

God is looking down to earth. He sees billions and billions of lost souls challenging Him to battle.

I think God will say to them, "You dare to come against me, the Almighty God. The God that gave you life. The God that gave you a soul. The God that gave you opportunities to be saved and eternal life in Heaven. You dare to challenge my authority and power?"

God will send fire out of Heaven and devour them in a flash.

The flesh of satan's army will fall off their bones before their body hits the ground.

....

Their eyes will withdraw backward into their eye sockets.

....

They will swallow their tongues.

....

The battle will be over in a minute. God does not drag this out, it's not even a challenge.

....

Read Rev. 20:10

....

Satan is cast into the lake of fire and brimstone.

....

This is the exact same place where the beast and false prophet were cast one thousand years earlier.

....

They will be tormented day and night forever and ever.

....

CHAPTER 11

SOULS AND THE BOOK OF LIFE

Exodus 32:33	And the Lord said unto Moses, Whosoever has sinned against Me, him will I blot out of My Book.
Psalms 69:28	Let them be Blotted out of the Book of the living, and not be written with the righteous.
Rev. 3:5	He who overcomes shall be clothed in white garments, and I will not blot out his name from the Book of Life; but I will confess his name before My Father and before His angels

These verses in the Bible suggest that God can blot out the names from the Book of Life of people that die without accepting Christ as their Savior.

There is a possibility that God intended to refer exactly that meaning.

As earthly humans we are faced with the responsibility of accepting or rejecting Christ as our Savior.

God is saying to the saved person, "I will not blot out your name from the Book of Life."

If we look at the verses with that interpretation, here is what it is saying to me:

God made a contract with mankind.

Heaven will keep the records of good and evil.

Every person's name is entered into the Book of Life at their conception.

There will be an age when that person becomes the age of accountability. If that person dies before the age of accountability, then their name remains in the Book of Life.

There will be a time-slot to note when a person becomes a Christian. The notation will be in the Book of Life.

After the age of accountability:
If there is never a date placed in the Christian time-slot before the person dies, then the Soul of the human has sealed their fate to an eternity without God. God will blot out the name of that person from The Book of Life. As unbelievers die, their names are removed from the book.

Rev. 20:12-15

12 And I saw the dead, small and great, stand before God; and the books were opened: and another book was opened, which is the book of life: and the dead were judged out of those things which were written in the books, according to their works.

13 And the sea gave up the dead which were in it; and death and hell delivered up the dead which were in them: and they were judged every man according to their works.

14 And death and hell were cast into the lake of fire. This is the second death.

15 And whosoever was not found written in the book of life was cast into the lake of fire.

At the final judgment, the Book of Life contains only the names of believers.

Only those saved by the Lord Jesus Christ have their names in the Book of Life. All others have been blotted out. The book now becomes "the Lamb's Book of Life."

....

No one can go to Heaven whose name is not in the Lamb's Book of Life.

....

If a person wants to protect themselves from the Great White Throne Judgment and Hellfire, they must place their trust and faith in Jesus Christ.

....

THE GREAT WHITE THRONE JUDGMENT

John 5:22	**For the Father judgeth no man, but hath committed all judgment unto the Son:**

Read Rev. 20:11-15

John sees a Great White Throne.

Him who sits on the throne is the person of the Godhead, Jesus Christ.

The Bible does not specify where the Great White Throne is located nor where the Judgment will take place. Heaven and earth fled away at the appearance of Christ on the Throne, so it will not occur on earth. It will not occur in Heaven because no sinner can enter God's presence.

The Great White Throne Judgment will take place somewhere in space between Heaven and earth.

God the Father will not judge, He has committed all judgment to His Son, Jesus Christ.

Christ is the Savior today, He will be Judge tomorrow.

John sees the dead, small and great stand before the Throne.

These are the unsaved souls that are facing judgment.

This Judgment is at the end of the Kingdom Age of one thousand years.

This is the final judgment of the unredeemed souls. The time for mercy and grace has passed.

The Record Books are opened. Another book is opened, which is the Lamb's Book of Life.

The Lamb's Book of Life is the Reservation Book that is maintained by God for those who believe in Jesus Christ. The Book contains the names of those with eternal life in Heaven.

The sea gives up the dead which are in it.

Death and hell delivers up the dead which are in them.

Every unredeemed person who ever lived will face the Great White Throne Judgment. They will be judged out of the things which are written in the Record Books. They will stand trial and be found guilty of violating God's law. They will be sentenced to unending torment in the lake of fire.

They will face:

A Judge,	*but no Jury.*
A Sentence,	*but no Appeal.*
A Prosecutor,	*but no Defender.*

They will face:

Justice,	*with no Forgiveness.*
Punishment,	*with no Mercy.*
Darkness,	*with no Light.*
Eternity,	*with no End.*

There is no hope of heavenly life for those that appear before the White Throne Judgment.

Every person is judged according to their works that are written in the Record Books.

Remember the story of Adam and Eve. God only commanded one thing of Adam and Eve, "Do not eat from the tree of Knowledge of Good and Evil."

From Adam and Eve, God expected obedience, devotion and faithfulness. What He got was disappointment from the couple that He created.

Sin began in the Garden of Eden, sin will end at the White Throne Judgment.

The book of Genesis tells the story of the beginning. The book of Revelation tells the story of the ending.

Adam and Eve chose their behavior and received their consequences.

John sees many standing before Jesus Christ to receive their judgment and their sentence of eternal torment in the lake of fire.

THE PEOPLE AT THE GREAT WHITE THRONE JUDGMENT

The people at the Great White Throne Judgment includes the wicked from all generations.

There will be those that died in the Flood.

There will be those that died when God destroyed Sodom and Gomorrah.

There will be those that did not receive Christ as their Savior during their lifetime.

If Adam and Eve did not repent of their sins and ask God for forgiveness, they will be standing at the front of the line of unredeemed souls.

There will be people that did not ask for and receive forgiveness for breaking the Ten Commandments.
> *(1) Thou shalt have no other gods before me.*
> *(2) Thou shalt not make unto thee any graven image.*
> *(3) Thou shalt not take the name of the LORD thy God in vain.*
> *(4) Remember the sabbath day, to keep it holy.*
> *(5) Honour thy father and thy mother.*
> *(6) Thou shalt not kill.*
> *(7) Thou shalt not commit adultery.*
> *(8) Thou shalt not steal.*
> *(9) Thou shalt not bear false witness.*
> *(10) Thou shalt not covet.*

There will be the Elders of the People, the Chief Priests and the Scribes that witnessed against Christ at the Crucifixion Trial.

There will be the religious leaders of Israel that condemned Christ and had Him crucified. The results will be the same for them at their trial. They announced Christ guilty, they will be judged by Christ at the White Throne Judgment and judged guilty.

There will be the soldiers that mistreated Christ at the Crucifixion. Also those that mocked Him, blindfolded Him and beat Him.

There will be the Centurion man that was being crucified for his crimes on another cross at the same time as Christ. He would not ask for forgiveness of his sins and he died and went to hell that same day.

There will be the false prophets of God's Word.

There will be the unredeemed men and women, kings and queens, rich and poor, young and old, educated and uneducated.

There will be billions and billions and billions of people that have sinned since Adam and Eve and have fallen into the devil's traps of sin.

Whosoever is not found written in the Lamb's Book of Life are cast into the eternal lake of Fire and Brimstone. There will be:
> *No Fire Departments.*
> *No Fire Stations.*
> *No Fire Trucks.*
> *No Fire Fighters.*
> *No Fire Suits.*
> *No Fire Extinguishers.*
> *No Fire Exits.*

There will be different degrees of punishment in hell. This judgment is to determine the degree of punishment. All suffer in the eternal fire but some will suffer more than others.

The antichrist and his evil followers will have their hell within hell and the punishment will be severe. The other unredeemed souls will have their own place of torment according to their punishment of Fire and Brimstone.

Hell is forever and ever.

This is the final judgment of the world.

Once the devil and his army receives their judgment, there will be no evil anywhere in the Universe.

EVERY TONGUE WILL CONFESS THAT JESUS CHRIST IS LORD

Rom 14:11-12   For it is written, As I live, saith the Lord, every knee shall bow to me, and every tongue shall confess to God.

                            So then every one of us shall give account of himself to God.

Roman 3:23   For all have sinned, and come short of the glory of God.

Even an atheist will give an account of himself to God.

An atheist is a person who disbelieves or lacks belief in the existence of God. There will be no atheists in hell. Because, every knee will bow and every tongue will confess that Christ is Lord of everything in Heaven, everything in earth and everything under the earth.

Even the atheist will confess that Jesus Christ is Lord.

Every person that ever lived will give an account to Christ of their personal life.

This is the second death.

Christ will not judge on the curve.

WARNING AGAINST HELL

Throughout the Bible, God's word is faithfully warning against hell.

Matthew 13:49-50   So shall it be at the end of the world: the angels shall come forth, and sever the wicked from among the just,

And shall cast them into the furnace of fire: there shall be wailing and gnashing of teeth.

Matthew 25:41   Then shall he say also unto them on the left hand, Depart from me, ye cursed, into everlasting fire, prepared for the devil and his angels.

Matthew 10:28   And fear not them which kill the body, but are not able to kill the soul: but rather fear him which is able to destroy both soul and body in hell.

Mark 9:43   And if thy hand offend thee, cut it off: it is better for thee to enter into life maimed, than having two hands to go into hell, into the fire that never shall be quenched.

Romans 3:23   For all have sinned, and come short of the glory of God.

John 3:16-18   For God so loved the world, that he gave his only begotten Son, that whosoever believeth in him should not perish, but have everlasting life.

For God sent not his Son into the world to condemn the world; but that the world through him might be saved.

He that believeth on him is not condemned: but he that believeth not is condemned already, because he hath not believed in the name of the only begotten Son of God.

Job 10:21-22   Before I go whence I shall not return, even to the land of darkness and the shadow of death;

A land of darkness, as darkness itself; and of the shadow of death, without any order, and where the light is as darkness.

The Bible describes Hell as a Literal Place.
> *A place of Agony.*
> *A place of Misery.*
> *A place of Sorrow.*
> *A place of Suffering.*
> *A place of Loneliness.*
> *A place of Damnation.*
> *A place of Punishment.*
> *A place of Eternal Pain.*
> *A place of Remembering.*
> *A place of Imprisonment.*
> *A place of Total Darkness.*
> *A place of Gnashing of Teeth.*
> *A place of Unquenchable Fire.*
> *A place of Never Ending Torment.*
> *A place of Eternal Conscious Punishment.*

....

Hell is also a place where there will be complete separation from God. Those who do not accept God's gift of repentance will be separated from God and His Love, Peace and Blessings forever and ever.

....

Romans 8:13-14   For if ye live after the flesh, ye shall die: but if ye through the Spirit do mortify the deeds of the body, ye shall live.

For as many as are led by the Spirit of God, they are the sons of God.

The Bible continues to have statements that death and damnation is waiting for those that choose to live the earthly way of life rather than in obedience to God.

SADDEST WORDS IN THE BIBLE

Matt. 7:22-23   22 Many will say to me in that day, Lord, Lord, have we not prophesied in thy name? and in thy name have cast out devils? and in thy name done many wonderful works?

23. And then will I profess unto them, I never knew you: depart from me, ye that work iniquity.

CHAPTER 12

A NEW HEAVEN AND A NEW EARTH

Revelation 21

Read Rev. 21:1-2

The first Heaven and the first Earth will pass away.

There is no more sea for it has disappeared, meaning that all the great oceans like the Atlantic and the Pacific are now gone.

There will continue to be lakes, streams and rivers.

John sees the Holy City, the New Jerusalem coming down out of Heaven from God.

John hears a great voice out of Heaven saying:

Rev. 21:3   **Behold, the Tabernacle of God is with men, and He will dwell with them, and they shall be His people, and God himself shall be with them, and be their God.**

Read Rev. 21:4

God will wipe away all tears from their eyes. There is:
No more death.
No more sorrow.
No more crying.
No more suffering.

No more sadness.
No more pain.
No more deafness.
No more blindness.
No more wants.
No more sin.
No more night.
No more sickness.
No more memory of the past.
For the former things have passed away.

Read Rev. 21:5-8

John sees God on the Heavenly Throne and God says to John, "Behold, I make all things new. Write, for these words are true and faithful."

John writes the words that God is quoting. God says,
"It is done. I am Alpha and Omega, the beginning and the end. I will give unto him the water of life. He who overcomes, will inherit all things and I will be his God and he will be my son."

"The fearful and unbelieving and the workers of the flesh, shall have their part in the lake which burns with fire and brimstone, which is the second death."

THE NEW JERUSALEM AND HOLY CITY

Read Rev. 21:9-11

One of the seven Angels which had delivered one of the vials of wrath upon the earth speaks to John saying, "Come and I will show you the Bride, the Lamb's wife."

The Angel takes John in spirit to a great and high mountain and shows him the great city, the Holy Jerusalem, descending out of Heaven from God.

Read Rev.21:12-15

The Holy City shows the radiance of God's Beauty.

....

The Holy City has four walls, each wall is 216 feet high. It has twelve gates, three gates on each wall.

....

Each of the twelve gates is managed by an Angel.

....

Each gate will have the name of one of the Twelve Tribes of Israel.

....

The wall of the city has twelve foundations. On each foundation is the name of one of the twelve Apostles.

....

One of the Angels had a golden reed to measure the city, the gates and the walls.

....

MEASUREMENTS OF THE HOLY CITY

....

Read Rev. 21:16-21

....

The Holy City is foursquare.

....

The length and the breadth and the height are equal measurements, about 1500 miles each.
The Holy City will be 1500 miles in length, 1500 miles wide, and 1500 miles high.

....

The walls are jasper.

....

The Holy City is pure gold.

....

The foundations of the walls are garnished with twelve precious stones and it is beauty upon beauty.

....

The twelve gates are twelve pearls.

....

The streets are pure gold.

....

THE GLORY OF THE NEW JERUSALEM

Read Rev. 21:22-27

There is no temple in the New Holy City because the Lord God Almighty and the Lamb are the Temple.

The City has no need for the sun or the moon for the Glory of God and the Lamb is the Light thereof.

The gates will never be shut and there will be no nights.

There is no fear in the City because Christ is the protector. This is a place of safety.

There is no sin in the City because the City is occupied by the Heavenly souls that have their names written in the Lamb's Book of Life.

Read Rev. 22:1-7

The same Angel which was showing John the Holy City, shows him more of the New Jerusalem.

John sees the river of water of life proceeding out of the Throne of God and of the Lamb.

The river of water of life is flowing down the street of pure gold.

On either side of the river is the tree of life.

The tree produces twelve different kinds of fruit every month.

The leaves of the tree are for the healing of the nations.

The saints of God will serve Him forevermore.

They will see His face and His name will be in their foreheads.

New Jerusalem will have no nights and no need for candles because God gives the light.

John hears the Angel say,
> *"Blessed is he who keeps the sayings of the prophecy of this Book."*

Read Rev. 22:8-11

When John sees and hears these things, he falls down before the Angel to worship him but the Angel said, "Do it not, for I am a prophet, worship God only."

Rev. 22:12   **And behold, I come quickly and My reward is with Me to give every man according as his work shall be.**

In this verse, 'I come quickly' is not meant to portray the 'time' of His Coming, but rather the 'suddenness' of His Coming.

Rev. 22:13   **I am Alpha and Omega, the beginning and the end, the first and the last.**

Rev. 22:14   **Blessed are they who do His Commandments that they may have the right to the Tree of Life and may enter into the City.**

Read Rev. 22:15-17

Jesus says,
"I am the root and the offspring of David and the bright and morning Star."

God, the Holy Spirit, gives a final invitation to the dying world.

The Holy Spirit and the Bride invites those that can hear the word, to come to the word.
Those that have a spiritual thirst can also come. And whosoever will, may take the water of life freely.

God gives a final Warning to man about the Book of Prophecy.

Read Rev. 22:18-19

No one is to add to the prophecy of the Bible.

No one is to take away from the prophecy of the Bible.

Reading Revelation can bless one's heart, or curse one's soul if he tampers with the Word of God.

The prophecy of the Bible testifies that Jesus Christ is Savior, and this fact is repeated again and again throughout the Bible.

Christ is the Lamb who was slain, and His blood washes away sin, and His blood alone provides entrance into the Holy City of God.

And so shall we ever be with the Lord forever and ever.

THE LAST PROMISE

Read Rev. 22:20

The Lamb says,
 "Surely I come quickly."

The message from God throughout the Bible is, "Come unto me."

The last words written by John in Revelation:

Rev. 22:21   **The Grace of our Lord Jesus Christ be with you all. Amen.**

As I close the book of Revelation, I close with these words:
God said it,
 I believe it,
  That settles it.

Summarization of the 'Day of the Lord' events

The Day of the Lord begins one second after the Rapture of the Church.

The world goes into the Seven Year Tribulation.

Christ will make His second trip to earth. He will not come to earth at the Rapture, He only comes in the clouds to get the saints. The second trip will be for a thousand years.

The Armageddon battle which results in damnation of the beast and the false prophet armies.

Satan is bound, restrained, controlled and placed in the bottomless pit for a thousand years.

Christ establishes peace and calmness on earth for a thousand years.

After the thousand years, satan is released from the bottomless pit and he goes after his second army to fight God.

God devours satan's army in a flash and cast satan into the Lake of Fire and Brimstone which burns forever and ever.

Great White Throne Judgment.

The present Heaven and earth passes away.

God creates a New Heaven and a New Earth.

The believers will be in the New Heaven forever and ever and the nonbelievers will be in hell forever and ever.

TEN THINGS A LOST PERSON WILL DISCOVER

"Ten Things a Lost Person Will Discover, One Second after Death."
is taken from the Book, "The Pain from the Death of a Spouse" by
Buddy Rogers ....
It is printed by permission. I gave myself permission to use this
article in this book.

Ten Things a Lost Person Will Discover, One Second after Death

1. One second after death the lost person will discover that ...
Death did not end it all.

2. One second after death the lost person will discover that ...
Satan has lied to them.

3. One second after death the lost person will discover that ...
Hell is real.

4. One second after death the lost person will discover that ...
Everyone will live eternally, in Heaven or Hell.

5. One second after death the lost person will discover that ...
God has a record of all their sins and He can see the sins of a lost person.

6. One second after death the lost person will discover that ...
They still have memories of their life.

7. One second after death the lost person will discover that ...
They are consumed by the works of their own hands.

8. One second after death the lost person will discover that ...
They missed the most important thing in life, knowing God.

9. One second after death the lost person will discover that ...
The opportunities they had to be saved are gone, and gone forever.

10 One second after death the lost person will discover that ...
Life's Short, Hell's Hot and Eternity's Long.

....

You may say or think, "If God is such a loving God, full of mercy and grace, then He will not send anyone to hell." When we humans think being sent to hell for our sins is unfair, not right and not merciful, then we are looking at the issue with our human perspective of fairness. God is the One who says what is right and wrong and what is fair, not we humans.

....

1 Peter 1:16   **Because it is written, Be ye Holy, for I am Holy.**

....

Holiness is the very nature of God's character. God wants us to be holy because He is Holy.

....

Holiness is perfection, purity, incorruptibility and the inability to sin, all of which are only possessed by God Himself.

....

1 John 4:16   **And we have known and believed the Love that God has to us. God is Love; and he who dwells in love dwells in God, and God in him.**

....

God's love is shown at the cross when God gave His Son to die for our sins. God cares about us and our wellbeing. His thoughts and love for us is why He doesn't want anyone to go to hell.

....

If we could get to Heaven by any means other than through Jesus Christ, then Jesus did not need to die on the cross. As sinners, we cannot do any earthly things that could justify us going to Heaven. God loves us enough that He established a way for us to have our sins forgiven through Jesus Christ His son.

....

Jesus is the only way to God. Jesus's death on the cross established a pathway to salvation.

....

If you want to escape the eternal judgment of God, you must put your trust in Jesus and what He did on the cross and in nothing else.

....

Without Jesus, there is no hope of escaping hell on the Day of Judgment.

Receive Jesus into your life, trust in Him alone, ask Jesus to forgive you of your sins, trust Him with all your heart and He will save you and deliver you from the Day of Judgment.

AS THE AUTHOR OF THIS BOOK

I cannot close the last chapter of this book without providing God's Plan of Salvation. It is not complicated. God does not ask us to jump through hoops or do crazy things. He only ask us to believe in Him, to trust Him, to ask Him for forgiveness, to accept Him as our Savior and to accept the gift of life that He is offering. These verses were selected from the Bible just for us earthly people.

Matt. 10:28
And fear not them which kill the body, but are not able to kill the Soul: but rather fear Him which is able to destroy both Soul and body in hell.

God is saying, don't worry about the person that can kill you by killing your body, but be concerned about the One that can destroy your body and your Soul in hell. Hell is for eternity, just as Heaven is for eternity.

Romans 6:23
For the wages of sin is death, but the gift of God is eternal life through Jesus Christ our Lord.

Romans 3:23
For all have sinned, and come short of the glory of God.

Even the most righteous person comes short of the Glory of God.

We must admit to ourselves that we are all sinners and in need of a Savior. God gave us a will and the freedom to choose.

If we choose to disobey God and do as we please, we commit sin and separation from Him. Christ paid for our sins at the cross and gave us a gift of eternal life in Heaven.

Romans 5:12
Wherefore, as by one man sin entered into the world, and death by sin; and so death passed upon all men, for that all have sinned.

The man spoken of in this verse is Adam. Adam and Eve sinned in the Garden of Eden and brought sin into the world. Mankind is born in sin. Death by sin is both spiritual death and physical death.

Romans 3:10   As it is written, There is none righteous, no not one.

This verse speaks for itself; we are all born as sinners.

John 3:16   For God so loved the world, that He gave His only begotten Son, that whosoever believeth in Him should not perish, but have everlasting life.

This shows the love God has for mankind. He gave His only Son to die for our sins.

Romans 5:8   But God commendeth his love toward us, in that, while we were yet sinners, Christ died for us.

Christ died for sinners because of His love for the human race.

1 John 1:8   If we say that we have no sin, we deceive ourselves, and the truth is not in us.

This speaks of our sinful nature. We are born into sin.

1 John 1:9   If we confess our sins, He is faithful and just to forgive us our sins and to cleanse us from all unrighteousness.

If we confess our sins with love, sincerity and truthfulness, God will faithfully forgive us of all our sins. Not some of our sins, but all of our sins.

John 6:47   Verily, verily, I say unto you, He who believes on Me hath everlasting life.

This is Everlasting Life that begins as soon as one accepts Christ as his or her Savior. It is promised to you but you don't have to wait for it. You get everlasting life immediately.

1 John 1:10   If we say that we have not sinned, we make Him a liar and His Word is not in us.

No human can claim sinless perfection because we're born with a sinful nature.

Romans 10:13   **For whosoever shall call upon the name of the Lord shall be saved.**

Any believer can come to Christ by means of the Cross.

Romans 10:9-10   **That if thou shalt confess with thy mouth the Lord Jesus, and shalt believe in thine heart that God hath raised Him from the dead, thou shalt be saved.**

                      For with the heart man believeth unto Righteousness; And with the mouth confession is made unto Salvation.

Man must confess that Jesus is Lord and Savior of mankind, that He died on the Cross and God raised Him from the dead. If you believe this, you can be saved.

Believing is a mode of thinking and believing Christ atoned for all sins. With the mouth confession is made unto salvation.

How you can accept Christ into your life.

+ *Admit your need to have Christ in your life.*
+ *Admit that you are a sinner.*
+ *Be willing to turn from your sins.*
+ *Be willing to repent of your sins. (Repent means that you feel sincere regret and sorrow about your wrongdoings.)*
+ *Believe that Jesus Christ died for you on the cross and rose from the grave.*
+ *Be willing to accept Christ by faith.*
+ *Through prayer, invite Christ into your life.*
+ *Receive Him as Lord and Savior.*

THE SALVATION PRAYER

Prayer is talking to God. The Savior is His son, Jesus. The only way to God, the only way to Heaven, the only way to salvation and the only way your sins can be forgiven is through Jesus. The Salvation prayer is expressing with your voice what you feel in your heart.

Your desire to be forgiven, your desire to change your life style, your desire to open your heart to Jesus should be expressed in your prayer. Jesus is waiting.

If you declare with your voice, Jesus is your Lord and you believe in your heart that God raised Him from the dead, you will be saved. For it is with your heart that you believe and are justified, and it is with your mouth that you profess your faith and are saved.

If you want Jesus in your life, just tell Him so. He is knocking at the door of your heart and is waiting for you to open the door and invite Him in. All opportunities for salvation are only on this side of death.

The Bible tells us how to live, how to be saved, how to accept Jesus as our Savior, how to change our lives, how to have eternal life, how to go to heaven, how to pray and how to have a relationship with the heavenly Father. The Bible is Life's Book of Instructions.

Your prayer is a conversation between you and God.

Here is an example of a Beginners Prayer that you may use to get the conversation started.

Dear Heavenly God,
I need your help. I know I am a sinner and I ask for your forgiveness. I ask you to forgive me of my many sins. I want you to be my Lord in the future. I believe your son Jesus lived on earth and died on the cross for my sins. I believe you raised Him from the dead. I want to trust you as my Savior and follow you as my Lord from this day forward. Guide my life and help me do your will. Help me become a strong and loving witness for you.

I ask these things in the name of Jesus.
Amen

✦ WHAT HAPPENS... ✦

Now that you have completed the most important decision in your life, you must now tell a church pastor of your decision. He will be thrilled and he has the information for the next step in your Christian growth. Christ is waiting for you.

....

May God save you and bless you for the rest of your earthly life and beyond. Remember, Love and Trust God the Father, God the Son and God the Holy Spirit, and you will be loved and blessed in Heaven for Eternity.

....

Printed in the United States
by Baker & Taylor Publisher Services